Prais

"*The Os*   our time: Why
are we   , and what can we
human   o cares about risk."
—Danie̲ ̲ ̲ ̲ ̲ ̲ ̲ ̲ ̲ ̲ ̲ ̲ ̲ ̲ ̲ ̲ ̲ ̲, ̲ ̲ ̲ ̲ ̲ ̲ ̲ ̲ ̲ ̲ ̲ ̲ ̲ ̲ ̲ ̲ ̲ ̲ ̲ the Nobel Prize in Economics and
author of *Thinking, Fast and Slow*

"At a time when we face looming short- and long-term risks as varied as
terrorism, cyberattacks, and climate change, this timely book diagnoses
the innate psychological barriers to effective disaster planning and
mitigation. Drawing on a variety of historical lessons and integrating
insights into psychology, the authors prescribe practical approaches to
disaster preparation. *The Ostrich Paradox* is a must-read, whether you
are protecting the nation or your own family."
— **Michael Chertoff, Former United States Secretary of
Homeland Security**

"*The Ostrich Paradox* is an essential, sobering read for anyone interested
in assessing and responding to tomorrow's hazards today. Robert Meyer
and Howard Kunreuther don't just help us understand why we don't
prepare for disasters as we should, they also show us how to alter those
behaviors and improve preparedness."
— **Alan Schnitzer, Chief Executive Officer, The Travelers
Companies, Inc.**

"Good things typically come in threes. In *The Ostrich Paradox*, however,
Meyer and Kunreuther skillfully distill a large body of recent
psychological insights on the barriers to action in the face of potential
peril into *four* steps of a behavioral risk audit and into *four* guiding
principles to ensure preventive action."
— **Elke U. Weber, Gerhard R. Andlinger Professor in Energy and
the Environment and Professor of Psychology and Public Affairs,
Princeton University**

THE
Ostrich
Paradox

WHY WE UNDERPREPARE
FOR DISASTERS

Robert Meyer and Howard Kunreuther

Wharton
DIGITAL PRESS
Philadelphia

Published by Wharton Digital Press
The Wharton School
University of Pennsylvania
3620 Locust Walk
2000 Steinberg Hall-Dietrich Hall
Philadelphia, PA 19104
Email: whartondigitalpress@wharton.upenn.edu
Website: http://wdp.wharton.upenn.edu/

Ebook ISBN: 978-1-61363-079-2
Paperback ISBN: 978-1-61363-080-8

Contents

To Barbara and Gail

Introduction
The Ostrich Paradox

When dawn broke on the morning of September 8, 1900, the people of Galveston had no inkling of the disaster that was about to befall them. The thickening clouds and rising surf hinted that a storm was on the way, but few were worried. The local weather bureau office, for its part, gave no reason to think otherwise; no urgent warnings were issued, no calls were made to evacuate. But by late afternoon it became clear that this was no ordinary storm. Hurricane-force winds of more than 100 miles per hour were soon raking the city, driving a massive storm surge that devoured almost everything in its path. Many tried to flee, but it was too late. By the next day, more than 8,000 people were dead, the greatest loss of life from a natural disaster in US history.[1]

Fast-forward to September 2008, when Hurricane Ike threatened the same part of the Texas coast, but this time being greeted by a well-informed populace. Ike had been under constant surveillance by satellites, aircraft reconnaissance, and land-based radar for more than a week, with the news media blasting a nonstop cacophony of reports and warnings, urging those in coastal areas to leave. The city of Galveston was also well prepared: A 17-foot-high seawall that had been constructed after the 1900 storm stood ready to protect the city, and government-flood insurance policies were available to residents who were at risk of property loss. Unlike in 1900, Texas residents really *should* have had little reason to fear. On their side was a century of advances in meteorology, engineering, and economics designed to ensure that Ike would, indeed, pass as a forgettable summer storm.

But for some reason it didn't quite work out that way. Warnings were issued, but many in low-lying coastal communities ignored them—even when told that failing to heed the warnings meant they faced certain death.[2] Galveston's aging seawall was breached in multiple places, damaging up to 80% of homes and businesses in the city. The resort communities to the north on the Bolivar Peninsula, which never saw the need for a seawall, fared even worse, witnessing almost complete destruction. And among the thousands of homeowners who suffered flood losses, only 39% had seen fit to purchase flood insurance.[3] In the end, Ike caused more than $14 billion in property damage and 100 deaths, almost all needless.

Why Are We Underprepared for Disasters?

The gap between protective technology and protective action illustrated by the losses in Hurricane Ike is, of course, hardly limited to Galveston or to hurricanes. While our ability to foresee and protect against natural catastrophes has increased dramatically over the course of the past century, it has done little to reduce material losses from such events.

Rather than seeing decreases in damage and fatalities due to the aid of science, we've instead seen the worldwide economic cost and impact on people's lives from hazards increase exponentially through the early twenty-first century, with five of the ten costliest natural disasters in history with respect to property damage occurring since 2005. While scientific and technological advances have allowed deaths to decrease on average, horrific calamities still occur, as in the case of the 230,000 people estimated to have lost their lives in the 2004 Indian Ocean earthquake and tsunami, the 87,000 who died in the 2008 Sichuan earthquake in China, the 160,000 who lost their lives in Haiti from an earthquake in 2010,[4] and the 8,000 fatalities that occurred in the 2015 Nepalese earthquake. Even in the United States, Hurricane Katrina in 2005 caused more than 1,800 fatalities, making it the third most deadly such storm in US history.

The purpose of this book is to explain this disconnect and to propose a solution. In part 1, we explore six reasons that individuals, communities, and institutions often underinvest in protection against low-probability, high-consequence events. In each chapter, we explore a specific bias that foils our ability to make good decisions in these types of situations. To illustrate the tragic shortcomings of our mind-sets, we share tragic stories from global disasters. These are the stories that motivated us to write this book and to offer a new approach to preparedness planning that will help to prevent such tragedies.

In part 2, building on this foundation, we describe how knowledge of these biases can be used to anticipate the kinds of errors that occur when people are faced with potential disasters and how we might avoid those errors. Our approach to preparedness planning provides individuals, firms, and policy makers with the means to anticipate the cognitive biases that often impede risk preparedness, so as to guide the design of more effective tactics that save lives and protect resources.

This new approach, the *behavioral risk audit*, seeks to reverse the traditional mind-set used when policies for protection are designed. Rather than proposing economic or engineering solutions to preparedness, and hoping that people will adopt them, the behavioral risk audit starts with an understanding of the psychological biases that inhibit adoption, and then proposes policies that work with, rather than against, our natural psychologies. As such, the intellectual foundation of the approach lies in the social sciences, notably behavioral economics and psychology, not engineering or natural science.

Why the Ostrich Paradox?

The title *The Ostrich Paradox* is a metaphor for the key idea we intend to communicate in this book. While ostriches are often characterized as hapless birds who bury their heads in the sand whenever danger approaches, they are, in fact, highly astute escape artists, birds who use their great speed to overcome their inability to fly. The core thesis of the book is that, much in the same way that ostriches are limited in their defensive actions because they cannot fly, we need to recognize that when making decisions, our biases are part of our cognitive DNA and are keeping us grounded, flightless. Still, we might be able to design and structure a suite of choice environments, incentives, and communication methods that allows human decision makers to overcome these biases when faced with future hazards. We suggest that we need to learn to be *more*, not *less*, like ostriches—hence the paradox—if we are to be better prepared for disasters.

PART I

Why We Underprepare
for Disasters

Chapter 1

A Tale of Two Cognitive Systems

Of the many stories of loss that emerged after Hurricane Sandy made landfall on the coast of New Jersey in late October 2012, few attracted more media attention than the tragedy of the Moore family. Dennis and Glenda Moore lived with their two children, ages two and four, in the Great Kills neighborhood of Staten Island, a borough of New York City.[5]

According to news reports, Dennis was working that evening, leaving Glenda to ride out the storm at home with the children. As afternoon transitioned into evening and the winds built in intensity, the Moores' home, like most in the area, lost its electricity. At that point, Glenda decided to load the children in the family sport utility vehicle and drive to her sister's house in the nearby borough of Brooklyn.[6]

While there are multiple routes that Glenda could have taken, the one she took was likely the most commonly traveled to Brooklyn: Father Capodanno Boulevard, which runs along the coast and leads directly to the Verrazano-Narrows Bridge. Under normal circumstances this would have been a short trip—twenty minutes, tops. But these were not normal circumstances—the National Hurricane Center had been repeatedly warning that Sandy's landfall would be accompanied by a storm surge of up to eleven feet above normal tide levels, something that would render most coastal roads impassable.[7] And indeed, as Glenda came within a mile of the bridge, Capodanno became engulfed by Sandy's rising storm surge, stalling her vehicle. She took the two children in her arms, left the car, and tried to wade to the safety of some houses she saw in the distance. She survived, but the children did not. A powerful wave swept them from her arms, and they were lost in the storm.[8]

While the loss of the Moore family was perhaps the most poignant that emerged after Hurricane Sandy, it was by no means unique; that same night, 20 others died from drowning in Staten Island alone.[9] What made these losses particularly devastating was that, unlike deaths in unforeseeable events such as terrorist attacks, in all cases the decision makers had ample time to contemplate how best to respond to the storm threat, and all had unprecedented amounts of information at their disposal to help guide them. All *thought* they were doing the right thing. But somewhere this measured calculus went terribly wrong.

The Two Cognitive Systems: Systems 1 and 2

If we want to understand why tragedies like this one can occur, and what we can do to prevent them, a starting point is to understand how people make decisions under conditions of risk and how these decisions can go awry. Today most psychologists agree that our brains make choices using two cognitive systems, one that governs automated and instinctive thoughts (such as those that take place when we jump away the instant we see a snake) and one that governs more controlled thoughts (such as those that allow us to decide what the best cure might be if the snake bites us).[10] In most contexts, these two systems, working in concert, allow us to navigate our day-to-day lives with ease using simple intuitions and rules of thumb, freeing up mental resources for more taxing deliberative calculations if needed.

To illustrate, consider driving to work. From the time we climb into the car to the time we arrive at our parking spot, we are faced with thousands of small decisions: whether to make a left or right turn when we get to the end of the driveway, whether to put on the brake when we see a car ahead slow down. If we had to deliberate over each of these during the course of a day, we would be overwhelmed; we just don't have the time. Fortunately, we don't have to reflect on these actions. Our brains automatically store previous successful decisions in long-term memory (e.g., the instinct to apply the brake when we see a taillight ahead light up), ready to be retrieved and executed whenever needed. This is what psychologists term our System 1 mode of thinking—it is fast, reflexive, and usually unconscious. The benefit of System 1 is that it frees up the part of our brains that is best at thoughtful calculation—what psychologists term System 2 thinking. As System 1 is guiding our hands and right foot while we cruise on a boring stretch of highway, System 2 is free to work on other, more effortful tasks that may have nothing to do with driving to work, such as strategizing about what to say at a staff meeting.

System 2 performs a second, perhaps even more important, function: controlling the influence that emotions and instincts have on our decisions. Hence, if during our drive to work we are suddenly startled by the unexpected sight of a disabled truck in the middle of the road, System 2 will (hopefully) jump into action, focusing our attention on the vehicle and suppressing intuitions that may not be helpful—such as the instinctive fear of driving on the shoulder of the road. As long as we have had some experience in situations like this, all will go smoothly. With some luck, the incident ends up being just a routine delay or detour in an otherwise mundane work commute.

Yet, here is the rub. As efficient as these intertwined systems may be for navigating the vast majority of situations we confront on a day-to-day basis, they perform very poorly when dealing with problems that are unfamiliar, complex, and temporally distant. In the case of Hurricane Sandy, many of those on Staten Island that night tried to use System 2 thinking to reason their way to the best protective decision, but they most likely lacked the necessary data: They knew too little about storm surges, too little about road conditions. In the face of this cognitive impasse, primal System 1 thinking took over— an instinct that proved fatal.

Catastrophe in the Atlantic:
When Two Systems Go Awry

Experts who have received extensive training in decision making are prone to the same kinds of mistakes. Consider the crash of Air France 447 in 2009, in which 228 people died when the plane went into a high-altitude stall over the tropical Atlantic. Recording boxes recovered after the crash revealed a cause that expert pilots found inexplicable: When a momentary equipment failure (the freezing of a speed sensor) caused the autopilot to disengage, the plane's less-experienced copilot, Pierre-Cédric Bonin, suddenly pitched the nose of the plane upward, which, at high altitude, caused the plane to lose lift and then stall.[11] The correct action in this situation would have been to make no change to the plane's controls or, if the plane did stall, to pitch the nose of the plane downward, not upward. For the next four minutes, as the plane descended to the sea, the cockpit recorder revealed the crew urgently trying to comprehend what was happening and how to remedy it. Only at the last second did the copilot tell the crew that he had the stick controlling the plane's pitch in the back rather than the forward position the whole time. The pilot and crew seemed to have been unaware of this.[12]

How could a trained pilot make such a high-stakes error? A plausible story is this: An essential part of pilot training is to teach reflexive (System 1) responses to potentially dangerous situations. Among these, perhaps the most fundamental is the pull-up maneuver: When a pilot hears an alarm indicating that the plane is descending too fast upon landing (or approaching other terrain), he or she is trained not to think but to react—that is, to allow the decision to be made by System 1, not System 2. For commercial airliners, this would involve accelerating the thrusters to pick up speed, as if on takeoff, and only then pitching the nose of the aircraft upward.[13] When Air France 447 was flying in the middle of the night with a (relatively) inexperienced copilot at the controls, the confusion that followed the indicator of the loss of airspeed and the automatic disengagement of the autopilot seemed to have triggered this automatic response: The copilot pulled the nose up. He was making decisions using System 1 instincts rather than System 2 deliberations.

Of course, after this happened, there was still time for him and two other crew members to use their System 2 abilities to diagnose the situation and enact a simple remedy, that is, pitch the plane downward, but this never happened. The crew had no experience solving the problem of an airworthy plane suddenly starting to descend with unreliable indicator gauges, so they had to construct an answer on the fly. But there were too many hypotheses to trace down, too little time to do it. The pilots overlooked the simplest of all explanations: The nose was pointed up.

Overcoming Our Innate Engineering: The Six Core Biases

If there is a common theme to the Moore family tragedy during Hurricane Sandy and the Air France 447 crash, it is this: When protective decisions go awry it is not because we lack the innate ability to make good decisions, but rather because these abilities are not well designed for dealing with rare threats for which we have little stored knowledge. When faced with low-probability, high-consequence events, System 2 tries to offer a remedy by evoking our powers of reason, but they are of little use if we lack the right data. Glenda Moore likely knew too little about storm surges; Pierre-Cédric Bonin may have known too little about high-altitude stalls. System 1 intuition thus tends to take control, but it often provides inappropriate advice—such as telling us to flee when frightened, or to pitch the nose of a plane upward when faced with a hazard.

Is there a remedy? At first blush, the prospects would seem bleak. The way we think, after all, is something that has evolved over millions of years, from a time when powers of deep deliberation were less important than reflexive reaction and instinctive anticipation. Our basic cognitive wiring is thus not something we can hope to change.

Still, there may be a way out. While preparedness errors *may* have many origins, research on disasters over the years suggests that most can be traced to the harmful effects of six systematic biases that reflect flaws in how we instinctively perceive risk (System 1 errors) and how we use these perceptions when making decisions (System 2 errors). These biases are:

1. **Myopia:** a tendency to focus on overly short future time horizons when appraising immediate costs and the potential benefits of protective investments;
2. **Amnesia:** a tendency to forget too quickly the lessons of past disasters;
3. **Optimism:** a tendency to underestimate the likelihood that losses will occur from future hazards;
4. **Inertia:** a tendency to maintain the status quo or adopt a default option when there is uncertainty about the potential benefits of investing in alternative protective measures;
5. **Simplification:** a tendency to selectively attend to only a subset of the relevant factors to consider when making choices involving risk; and
6. **Herding:** a tendency to base choices on the observed actions of others.

While we may not be able to alter our cognitive wiring, we *may* be able to improve preparedness by recognizing these specific biases and designing strategies that anticipate them. Over the next six chapters we will explore the nature of each of these biases in turn.

Chapter 2

The Myopia Bias

In the 1990s the director general of Thailand's department of meteorology was a man named Dr. Smith Dharmasaroja. Smith oversaw the day-to-day workings of the country's weather monitoring systems, a job that included coordinating with regional meteorological offices and, of course, producing the country's daily weather forecasts. He also had responsibility for overseeing emergency responses to a hazard that was not particularly weather related: tsunamis. What made this job challenging was that while countries around the Pacific had had a coordinated tsunami warning system in place since the late 1940s, no comparable system existed in the Indian Ocean, and Thailand itself was ill-prepared should one strike. The country had the technology to detect earthquakes, but no way of knowing whether a quake had produced a tsunami or, if it had, of alerting threatened coastal towns. In 1998, Smith urged officials in the various coastal provinces to install a network of sirens, but the advice fell on deaf ears.[14] Sirens do not come cheap, officials argued, and installing such devices could have a dampening effect on tourism. After all, who wants to be reminded of tsunami risk while on holiday? Thailand eventually found a fix for the problem the next year, but it was not the one Smith had recommended: They replaced him as director general.

The cost of this decision was realized six years later, when a 9.3-magnitude earthquake propagated a massive tsunami throughout the Indian Ocean region. When seismometers in Bangkok recorded the quake, a meeting of the country's meteorologists was hastily called to decide whether to declare a tsunami emergency. The group was unsure what to do. What if they ordered evacuations only to have the event prove a false alarm? There could be professional repercussions. In the end, they decided to do nothing. It was, of course, no false alarm; within the hour, more than 5,000 would be dead along Thailand's coasts, with more than 230,000 dead across 14 countries bordering the Indian Ocean.[15]

The failure to see value in investing in relatively low-cost warning systems throughout the Indian Ocean in advance of the 2004 tsunami illustrates perhaps the most crippling of all biases that hinder decisions to invest in protection against low-probability, high-consequence events: myopia, or the tendency to focus on the short-term rather than the long-term implications of our actions. While the 2004 tsunami is a particularly acute example, similar stories of nearsightedness could be told for almost all disasters. The flooding of New Orleans that occurred during Hurricane Katrina in 2005 could have been prevented had it not been for years of procrastination by the US Army Corps of Engineers and the state of Louisiana in completing and maintaining a well-designed levee system that was first proposed in 1965.[16] Likewise, in 2010, federal courts concluded that the 2008 Gulf oil spill could have been averted had BP not embraced a corporate culture that prioritized short-term gains in minimizing cost over long-term gains in safety.[17] In both cases there were opportunities to invest in protective action that could have reduced major losses, but these were bypassed, as the more immediate short-term concerns dominated long-term needs.

Why, and How, We Are Myopic

What makes myopia a particularly difficult bias to overcome is that, like all the biases we discuss in this book, it is a good bias to have for most of the decisions we make on a day-to-day basis. After all, the present usually matters more than the future. If your house catches fire, the first order of business should be to escape and call the fire department (in that order), not worry about such long-run concerns as how many weeks it will take to get an insurance settlement. When things go awry, however, our brains sometimes take this notion too far. Rather than just underweighing future consequences, we sometimes ignore them altogether, or apply instinct in situations where it does more harm than good.

Neuropsychologists who have studied mistakes when trading off short-term and long-term consequences argue that the culprit often lies in our neurology—the fact that our brains treat rewards that are immediately present quite differently from those that lie in the imagined future.[18] To illustrate, consider a dieter who is doing his best to avoid sugary foods, but who is suddenly tempted by one of his favorite desserts. The part of his brain that handles analysis and reason, primarily the prefrontal cortex, tries to jump into action, reminding him of the future rewards that will come from resisting temptation. Unfortunately, it will likely be beaten to the punch by the more primitive limbic system of his brain, which handles such basic, and impulsive, emotions as hunger. When pitted against each other, the latter invariably wins out, and the dieter succumbs to the dessert. The next day, of course, when the limbic urges have long faded, he deeply regrets the misstep and laments his lack of self-control. By then, of course, it is too late; myopia has taken its toll.

Economists, too, have had a long-standing interest in studying myopia, though with a different focal point: measuring how far preferences for short-term outcomes depart from what would be expected if people were thinking deliberatively when discounting future outcomes.[19] As an economist sees it, people should trade off the prospect of receiving a reward now, versus in the future, in the same way that a banker assesses the time value of money. For example, if your bank generously offers you a 20% annual return on savings, you should feel the same about having $100 in cash in your pocket today versus having a check for $120 mailed to you in a year. Perhaps not surprisingly, however, experiments on how people actually make intertemporal trade-offs find that intuitive assessments of the time value of money bear little resemblance to those that would be made by a banker. Rather, people routinely engage in what is termed *hyperbolic discounting*, where they demand far more compensation for short-term delays of gratification than could be explained by such rational considerations as interest rates.[20] A hyperbolic discounter would be loath to give up $100 in cash today for $120 in a year, but would be willing to wait for the larger amount if the initial $100 were itself delayed—for example, $100 in a month versus $120 in a year and a month. To a banker, however, the two scenarios are equivalent.

One of the important implications of hyperbolic discounting is that it helps explain why out-of-pocket expenses are often given excessive weight when people consider investing in protective action. For example, prior to the 2004 tsunami disaster, it was well known that the cost of installing a warning system throughout the Indian Ocean would be relatively small, particularly when scaled against the number of lives that were subsequently lost: about $200 million for the initial construction and $1 million a year for maintenance.[21] It was thus hard for people to fathom why countries had been unable to see the clear merits of such a relatively small shared expenditure. Hyperbolic discounting, however, helps offer a psychic explanation. While regional finance ministers might well have acknowledged that tsunamis posed a distant threat, paying to be alerted to them would have required overriding a deeply ingrained focus on that which was immediate: the bureaucratic challenge of raising the money, putting aside spending for things with more tangible benefits, and increasing the chances of getting reelected if they were running for office. Much like the dieter who succumbs to a tempting dessert, in the psychic war between the short run and the long run, the officials let the former easily win out.

Hyperbolic discounting also helps explain another common feature associated with taking protective action: the prevalence of procrastination.[22] One of the paradoxical properties of hyperbolic discounting is that one could be averse to spending money for protection today, but see it as a wise investment for tomorrow. To illustrate, consider a homeowner who is told that if she invests $10,000 in flood proofing, she could receive a discount of $2,500 on her annual insurance premium. If she has no immediate plans to move, this would of course be a great deal; not only would the improvements pay for themselves in four years, but afterward she would reap a nice monetary return on the investment.[23] Unfortunately, if she is a hyperbolic discounter, this could still be a hard pill to swallow: She would be weighing an immediate cash outlay of $10,000, a highly tangible immediate loss, against a far-less-tangible stream of future gains. But if she delays her decision to invest until next month, this same $10,000 outlay would be imagined more tolerable. The reason is that, as a *future* expense, it would no longer be subject to the psychic inflation that occurs when it is immediate and out of pocket. Of course, a month from now the $10,000 expenditure would once again be seen as aversive, so she would succumb to a continuous cycle of good-faith postponements, which would cause the flood-proofing never to be undertaken. In short, the high upfront costs of protective investments will always seem as more palatable when viewed as something to be done tomorrow.

Others Sources of Myopia: Temporal Construal

In recent years, psychologists interested in intertemporal choice have provided more detailed explanations for why we tend to be so present-focused. One such mechanism is Trope and Liberman's *temporal construal theory*, an account of how people differentially attend to the attributes of options when decisions are to be made for today as opposed to the future.[24] The core notion of construal theory is that when we make present-oriented decisions, such as whether to pay today for flood proofing, our minds are drawn to the more concrete attributes of the problem at hand, such as the physical act of calling a contractor and the displeasure of writing a check. In contrast, when that same decision is imagined for the future, our minds are drawn to the problem's more abstract aspects, such as the feelings of safety and virtue that the payment would afford. As such, construal theory's explanation for why we are myopic differs in an important way from that provided by hyperbolic discounting: Under construal theory, people act myopically *not* because they give less weight to consequences per se, but rather because of a change in which consequences they focus on when thinking about the present versus the future.

As an example, consider the case of hurricane evacuations. In one of the author's field studies of evacuation intentions prior to Hurricane Sandy in 2012, coastal residents were asked 48 hours before the storm's expected landfall the likelihood that they would evacuate if they were ordered to do so.[25] At that point there was a reasonably high level of intended compliance; approximately 55% said they would if the order came. But when an evacuation was actually ordered just 12 hours later, there was a paradoxical dip in stated compliance, and it stayed low until the storm's landfall— despite Sandy's becoming stronger and the likelihood of landfall more real. Why the decrease? Construal theory provides a natural explanation. At 48 hours, when the prospect of evacuation stood as a hypothetical future threat, it was easy for residents to indicate their intention to comply, as their minds would have been focused on the abstract emotional feelings associated with taking steps to leave the area: the peace of mind that would come from staying out of harm's way and the mental satisfaction from acting responsibly.

Yet 12 hours later, when the threat became imminent, the mental situation radically changed; now the focus was on the concrete challenges that come with evacuation: finding lodging that will take pets, deciding what items to take, and what time to leave. Faced with such logistical concerns, the prospect of evacuation now became far less attractive, so many residents took a wait-and-see attitude, imagining that such concrete issues would be of less concern hours later (when, again, the abstract virtues of leaving would have been more mentally salient). In the end, it was estimated that only 19% of residents in areas under mandatory evacuation orders actually evacuated.

Recap: The Challenge of Myopia

Decisions to invest in protective measures require powers of foresight. Whether it is a city's decision to build a protective seawall, a homeowner's decision to flood proof her home, or a coastal resident's decision on whether to evacuate from a hurricane, all require up-front investments to achieve delayed (and usually uncertain) benefits. Unfortunately, one of our greatest weaknesses as decision makers is that our intuitive planning horizons are typically shorter than that needed to see the long-run value of such investments. While we might appreciate the need for a seawall or a safer home, our myopia imposes a crippling handicap on our ability to adopt them. We either do not see the value of the investments or we procrastinate in adopting them, mistakenly believing that the future versions of ourselves will be more far-sighted than the current version.

Of course, if the perceived consequences of *not* having protection are severe enough, myopia can be overcome. One would think, for example, that residents of Galveston, where 8,000 people died at the turn of the century, would have known better than anyone the virtues of proactive investments in hurricane preparedness, and that investors who suffered in the 2008 and 2009 real estate and equities collapse would have seen the virtues of safeguards that curbed excessive speculation. Unfortunately, as challenged as we are in thinking about the future, we are not any better at learning what we should from the past.

In the next chapter we take up the companion bias to myopia: historical amnesia.

Chapter 3

The Amnesia Bias

The city of Miyako lies on the northeast coast of Japan, about a five-hour train ride on the Shinkansen high-speed railway from Tokyo. While most of its income derives from commercial fishing, in recent years Miyako has grown in popularity as a jumping-off spot for visiting some of Japan's most spectacular points of natural beauty. On March 11, 2011, however, the city became known for something far more tragic. At 2:46 p.m. one of the strongest seismic events ever recorded struck the city, the great Tohoku earthquake. The quake was centered in the Pacific, about 200 miles to the southeast, and registered 9.0 on the Richter scale—63 times stronger than the earthquake that destroyed San Francisco in 1906.

At first, Miyako withstood the blow. Japan had seen numerous earthquakes, and as a result it had some of the world's most stringent building codes. While there was some initial damage, the Tohoku quake was precisely the kind of event the city had been designed to survive. But the city was not built to survive what followed. Shortly after 3:00 p.m., a 129-foot tsunami, the second largest ever recorded, came funneling up Miyako's bay, destroying everything in its path.[26] When the water had subsided, more than 4,000 structures (most of the city) lay in ruin. Most tragically, while many were able to seek safety as the tsunami rolled in, 420 residents lost their lives.[27]

Yet this wasn't Miyako's or the area's first earthquake or tsunami. Centuries-old stone markers line the Iwate Prefecture coastline. Many of these monuments were erected shortly after earlier earthquakes and tsunamis devastated the area. One such catastrophe destroyed the city in 1933, killing 42% of the city's population.[28] One monument, inscribed in old kanji, reads, "High dwellings are the peace and harmony of our descendants. Remember the calamity of the great tsunamis. Do not build any homes below this point."[29]

The hope was that a warning could be given to those who would resettle in the area. Despite these warnings, though, as the past earthquakes and tsunamis fell into distant memory, the same port valley was rebuilt, only to have the tragic cycle repeat itself less than a century later.

This chapter explores the flip side of the myopia bias that we discussed in the last chapter: Not only do we seem poorly equipped to consider the future when making decisions, but we also seem to have a hard time fully learning lessons from the past, which is why, it seems, disasters always seem destined to repeat themselves.

Limits to Learning about Protection

One of the most remarkable of all human skills is our ability to learn to perform highly sophisticated tasks using nothing more than trial and error. Consider, for example, how we learn to ride a bicycle. When we try to ride, but fall, the resulting pain sends an unambiguous signal to our brains that we have done something wrong, and we should take a different action next time. If we then manage to pedal a few feet without falling, our brains tag these actions as a success and urge us to keep repeating them. Of course, if the initial pain is too severe, we might choose never to get back on the bike, but there is a built-in fix for that: Our memories for pain tend to be short-lived, particularly when they can be replaced by something more positive. In time, this instinctive cycle of repeating actions that yield good outcomes, and forgetting the pain of missteps, allows us to be decent cyclists so we can navigate the neighborhood with our friends.

Yet here's the rub: As beneficial as this intuitive approach to learning may be for acquiring most day-to-day skills, it can backfire when it is used to discover the value of investing in protection against low-probability, high-consequence events. The reason is simple: In such contexts, successful learning requires us to *reverse* the natural tools we use to acquire skills in other domains. Unlike bike riding, learning to see value in protection against rare events requires long, not short, memories for past pains and mistakes. It also requires us to see value in costly actions that carry few observable rewards. A successful protective act, after all, is one that leaves our lives unchanged; the benefit lies only in losses that might have occurred but did not. Because this cognitive reversal is hard to achieve, our normal tools for trial-and-error learning often have the effect of teaching us to *avoid*, not invest in, protection.

The Harmful Effects of Short Memories

It is often observed that history is inevitably prone to repeat itself, and perhaps nowhere is this truer than in disasters. People resettle in floodplains, stock market crashes come in cycles, and careless drivers suffer repeated crashes. Each time such an event occurs, one hears pledges to take steps to ensure that the adverse event never occurs again, but inevitably it does—something routinely attributed to short memories.

It is important to emphasize, however, that if disasters often repeat themselves, it is usually *not* because past disasters themselves have been forgotten. Quite the contrary: People often have quite clear memories of past disasters (such as the 9/11 attacks), and communities often make efforts to keep memories of past disasters alive through monuments, such as the warning tablets that line the hills above Miyako. What *is* quickly forgotten, however, is the *hedonic impact* of past losses, the acute sense of tragedy that one feels when seeing one's house destroyed, or the fear one feels in the immediate wake of a terrorist attack. We suggest that it is the fading of these emotional drivers, not objective memories for the disasters themselves, that causes attitudes toward protection to become increasingly lax with time.

A case in point is the story of the Galveston Seawall and the destruction of the Bolivar Peninsula during Hurricane Ike in 2008, the disaster with which we began this book. After the 1900 catastrophe, the surviving residents of Galveston eschewed the natural instinct to abandon the city and rebuild elsewhere. Instead, they used their own money to construct a massive seawall around the city that was 17 feet high and 16 feet wide at its base—high enough to ward off the tides of all but the most extreme hurricanes.[30] Even more remarkable, residents also funded raising the elevation of the entire city from 2 to 18 feet above sea level.

The protective investments worked. Over the next century the Texas coast was repeatedly hit by hurricanes, some stronger than the 1900 storm, but none imposed more than minor damage on Galveston. And lest residents somehow attribute the lack of losses to a belief that the city was inherently immune to storms, on the 100th anniversary of the storm a monument was installed on top of the wall to remind residents and visitors why the wall was there.

Yet the seawall came with one aesthetic cost, one that, for many, increasingly trumped the advantages of safety it afforded: the loss of the city's natural beach. As the neighboring metropolis of Houston grew, and as wealthier residents looked for places to build vacation homes, the unsightly seawall (and by extension, the protection it afforded) was something to be avoided rather than sought. The unprotected coasts just north and south of the city were thus rapidly developed. Of course, it would be just a matter of time before another major hurricane struck the area, and in 2008 one did: Hurricane Ike. While there indeed was damage in the city proper, it was nothing compared to the complete destruction that occurred on the Bolivar Peninsula, just to the north, which had been highly developed.

In the weeks that followed, it seemed as though the only sensible remedy for the Bolivar Peninsula was to abandon it. To this end, the federal government offered a buy-back program to more than 1,000 residents who had lost their homes in the storm, with the intention that there be no rebuilding there. Still, memories prove short. Rather than walking away, by 2010 the empty lots that were once seen as testaments to the inherent risk posed by the location were now seen as cheap buying opportunities, and a new building boom ensued.[31] The disaster cycle was poised to begin anew.

When Experience Teaches Us to Take on Risk

As beneficial as trial-and-error learning may be as a means for teaching us how to perform day-to-day tasks, it also has a dark side; when applied to learning about the value of protection, it sometimes teaches us to *avoid* rather than seek the behaviors that would most ensure our safety. The reason is that, in these contexts, rewards often become flipped such that it is the actions that are the best for us that go unrewarded, while those that are bad for us get reinforced.

Take the decision to purchase insurance as a form of protection. In the wake of Hurricane Katrina, the National Flood Insurance Program witnessed a significant rise in the number of flood policies issued, only to see that number drop to pre-Katrina levels three years later.[32] While fading memories of Katrina likely played a role in many of these cancellations, so, too, did the fact that the insurance, as most people discovered, carried little reward. While holding a policy may have provided a sense of mental comfort, that was a luxury many felt they could ill afford, given more critical (and rewarding) household expenses. It hard to convince people that "the best return on an insurance policy is no return at all."

This same tendency for protective actions to wane when there is no reinforcement also helps explain the reluctance of individuals to employ protective measures even after they have incurred the costs of purchasing them. Consider, for example, the failure of many coastal homeowners to put up storm shutters in advance of hurricanes. Data from a recent unpublished study by one of the authors revealed that as Hurricanes Earl and Irene were approaching the North Carolina Outer Banks in 2010 and 2011, only 55% of residents who owned shutters said they intended to put them up when warnings were issued. What made this result particularly surprising was that there was little evidence that this failure was due to misplaced optimism that the storms might miss them; when residents were asked to judge the probability that their homes would be affected by hurricane-force winds, the probabilities they gave were considerably *higher* than the objective probabilities communicated by the National Hurricane Center—often by orders of magnitude.

Rather than teaching them the value of shutters, prior experience with hurricanes seems to have done just the opposite. Storm shutters, for all their benefits, are not easy to put up; nor are they easy to take down, so there is a tangible cost for installing them unnecessarily. Of course, there is a far *larger* cost for failing to put them up should a hurricane make landfall in the vicinity of one's house, but that is an outcome that few residents had experienced. In addition, residents may know that hurricane warnings are normally issued over larger areas than those that end up experiencing actual storm conditions. Hence when warnings are issued for a given area, shutters will not have been needed most of the time.[33]

The prudent homeowner who puts up the shutters for a storm that misses his area recalls the time and effort of installing them and then having to take them down, whereas the neighbor who avoids taking this preventive measure remembers the relaxing day spent at the beach and how good it felt to be an expert forecaster. Moreover, even if the storm were to make landfall in a homeowner's area, the protective benefits of the shutters can only be imagined in advance. In other words, the homeowner has to construct a scenario that characterizes the additional damage that *would* have occurred to his house had the shutters *not* been installed.

In summary, when we are faced with a decision as to whether to put up storm shutters, or to invest in most protective measures, a battle is waged between two psychological forces: the *instinct* not to take action now, based on years of disaster-free experience, and the *knowledge* that we probably should incur the cost of undertaking protection in advance of a disaster based on the likelihood that it might occur. In the case of shutters purchased for the property, the homeowner may have heard warnings that hurricane winds are likely in his area and that it would be prudent to install them. Unfortunately, in many of these battles it is instinct that emerges as the winner over knowledge.

The Fear of Crying Wolf

Up until this point we have provided what might seem to be a bleak portrait of our ability to see value in taking steps now to reduce losses from disasters, particularly if experts issue warnings. Learning is impeded by two forces: a tendency to quickly forget the emotional impact of losses and a tendency for protective actions to go unrewarded far more often than they are rewarded. While both of these can be harmful, a case can be made that the second is the more worrisome, as it implies that there may be limits as to how effective we can be in warning people of looming threats, even when those threats are on the horizon as illustrated by hurricane forecasts.

Here is the logic: By definition, the likelihood and impact of a disaster cannot be predicted with certainty, so warnings are given to more people than will actually experience damage. While most would agree that it is better to be safe than sorry, doing so carries the risk of having the "cry wolf" effect, a reference to Aesop's famous fable of the shepherd boy who repeatedly fooled villagers into believing that a wolf was attacking his flock, only to be unable to recruit aid once the real threat materialized. The reluctance of North Carolina residents to put up shutters might be explained in these terms—feeling that one's effort is wasted when the storm does not materialize and deciding not to heed the next warning.

Other examples are easy to find. Car alarms are widely ignored when they go off, motorists ignore maintenance reminders on their car dashboards, and fire alarms are frequently ignored when residents or employees are asked to leave their homes or offices. Even single encounters with false alarms can trigger the cry wolf effect; in 2007 a false tsunami warning in Aceh, Indonesia, induced such great trauma among residents that they forcibly disabled the system.[34]

But there is a stroke of good news here. While cry wolf effects are quite real in some cases, the bias is far from universal. As an example, in the summer of 1996, residents of North Carolina were subject to two hurricane landfalls in quick succession, both of which triggered evacuation orders: Bertha in late July and Fran in mid-September. Whereas Bertha proved to be a false alarm, Fran was a more serious threat. In a post-storm survey of coastal residents, Kirstin Dow and Susan Cutter found that the false alarm of Bertha did little to impede evacuation rates for Fran (which were much higher), and that only 2% of respondents indicated that they would be less inclined to evacuate because the actual impact of the storms proved less than they had feared.[35]

The fortuitous recollection of a past false alarm in this case likely had two sources. First, unlike false car or fire alarms, in both cases the hurricane threats in North Carolina were quite real; they both hit the coast as forecast but with a bit less fury than was feared. Second, in the same way that people quickly forget the emotional impact of past disaster losses, they also quickly forget the emotional impact of having taken protective actions that proved unneeded. As Fran was approaching, coastal residents seemed willing to believe that the current threat was indeed the "big one," and this signal swamped faded memories of past warnings that proved to be overblown.

We should caution, however, that the cry wolf effect could manifest itself in other ways, even when warnings are successful in triggering action. A good example of this is the Crescent City, California, tsunami in 1964 that took the lives of eleven residents.[36] The town's sheriff, the official responsible for issuing evacuation orders after a tsunami alert, had come under criticism the previous year for ordering an evacuation of the coastal area after an earthquake advisory. When a similar advisory arrived late on the night of March 28, he hesitated, fearing repercussions should this be another false alarm. It was only when it became clear that the risk this time was real, moments before a 21-foot tidal wave swamped the city, that an evacuation was ordered, but by then it was too late.

Recap: Why We Have Trouble Learning from the Past

In the wake of almost all major disasters there will be news articles highlighting how the impending catastrophe could have been foreseen from prior experience. When Hurricane Katrina flooded the city of New Orleans in 2005, much of the blame was directed at policy makers who had been remiss in maintaining the city's vital levees, which implies a collective amnesia as to why the levees had been constructed in the first place. When Hurricane Sandy wrought devastation along the Northeast coast in 2012, some tried to excuse the lack of preparedness by claiming that the storm was an unforeseen quirk of climate change, overlooking historical experience: The Northeast coast is prone to a major hurricane hit every fifty years or so. And of course, those who invested in the World Trade Center in July 2001 seemed oblivious to the risks the buildings posed, despite their having been the target of a terrorist attack less than a decade before 9/11.

In this chapter, we argued that these seeming acts of forgetting are the result of two forces that, acting in tandem, make investments in protective action difficult to sustain. The first force is emotional: While we might well have good objective memories for past catastrophes, memories of the emotions that accompanied them tend to fade quickly—and this emotional reaction is critical to motivating action. The second force is positive reinforcement: Costly protective actions, when undertaken, are rarely positively reinforced. A homeowner who lets her flood insurance policy lapse in order to afford a new television set is much more likely to feel good about this purchase than to regret not having maintained her insurance coverage should she suffer damage from a flood next year. In essence, when it comes to safety, the reward structures become flipped from what they are in most aspects of life: The actions that are the most beneficial to us in the long run get punished, while those that are the least beneficial get rewarded.

In the next chapter, we take up a cognitive limitation that might be seen as the underlying currency of both myopia and amnesia: a tendency to have distorted perceptions of risk. While these distortions can cut both ways—sometimes we overestimate risk, sometimes underestimate—for decisions to invest in protective action, the latter is clearly the larger concern. The factors that drive such biased perceptions will be our next focus.

Chapter 4

The Optimism Bias

In the rarified air of New York City real estate moguls, few stood taller in 2001 than Larry Silverstein. Over the years, Larry had assembled an impressive portfolio of marquee properties. In late July, he was poised to acquire the crown jewel of his collection: the twin towers of the World Trade Center (WTC). After months of bargaining, he had finally secured from the Port Authority of New York and New Jersey, a 99-year lease priced at $3.2 billion, an amount that included $14 million of his own money.[37]

It was known that the buildings carried risk. Just eight years earlier, terrorists detonated 1,500 pounds of explosives in the basement of the North Tower, killing six and injuring more than 1,000, and the years since had seen a growing threat of terrorist attacks worldwide. In addition, a report commissioned just before the Silverstein acquisition highlighted a long list of things that could go wrong with the buildings, one being the possibility of an airliner crashing into one or both of the towers.[38] Still, whatever risks the WTC posed, they were not enough to dissuade Silverstein from purchasing the buildings or dissuade tenants from renting office space. Just the year before, for example, the WTC experienced an all-time high occupancy rate.[39] Whatever the risks of acquiring the WTC, all the relevant parties saw them as small relative to the financial upside.

The risks posed by the WTC also did not serve as a barrier to Silverstein's securing insurance coverage. When he acquired the buildings, a consortium of 22 insurers provided him with $3.55 billion in coverage should the WTC suffer any future damage.[40] What was most interesting about these policies, however, was not their existence but how they were written. Despite the history of the buildings as a target for terrorism, when drawing up the contract, insurers were content to lump losses due to a future terrorist attack under a standard "all-other perils" clause, meaning that this risk was not priced independently when the premium was determined. In essence, insurers saw the chance of losses from another terrorist attack as sufficiently remote that it could be pooled with a wide range of other difficult-to-imagine events, such as the towers being struck by an errant meteor.

Of course, soon after Silverstein signed the final paperwork, the unthinkable *did* happen: On the morning of September 11, 2001, terrorists flew two commercial airliners into the towers, causing both to collapse, killing more than 2,700 people. Silverstein declared his intention to rebuild, though he and his insurers became embroiled in a multiyear dispute over whether the attack constituted one event or two. A settlement was reached in 2007, with insurers agreeing to pay out $4.5 billion.[41] The eventual combined loss of the disaster and the cost of rebuilding greatly exceeded the insurance settlement.

Silverstein's misfortunes, however, did not end with the 9/11 attack. On December 11, 2008, a financier named Bernard Madoff was arrested in New York on charges of securities fraud. For more than a decade, Madoff had been running an investment securities firm that promised selected investors a high rate of return with virtually no variance, one that by 2008 claimed more than $65 billion in paper assets.[42] The firm, however, turned out to be a Ponzi scheme, one that would turn out to inflict billions of dollars in losses for hundreds of his clients. When the news media released a list of famous celebrities and investors who had been victimized by the scam, one familiar name again stood out: Larry Silverstein.[43] A low-probability event had once again taken its toll.

While vastly different in nature and scope, the 9/11 attacks and the Madoff scandal have one thing in common: Both illustrate the catastrophic outcomes that can occur when one does not fully consider all the consequences of foreseeable risks. While it would have been impossible to put a precise probability on the chance of a terrorist attack prior to 9/11, or the odds that Bernard Madoff was running a Ponzi scheme, in both cases information was available to officials that, if properly attended to, might at least have lessened the scale of the losses. After the Madoff scandal, for example, the Securities and Exchange Commission conceded that it had information indicating that a fraud was in the works up to *nine years* before the event,[44] and in the wake of the World Trade Center disaster, the 9-11 Commission pointed to numerous similar intelligence failures.[45]

In both cases Silverstein's decisions were fueled by psychological factors that should have played little (if any) role: the emotional lure of winning a bidding war for the WTC purchase and the trust that Madoff would never undertake a Ponzi scheme.

In this chapter, we try to explain why individuals and organizations often err when forming assessments of the likelihood of rare events—why Larry Silverstein was one of many who underestimated the risk of a terrorist attack on 9/11, and why he and so many other investors failed to recognize that something was not right with Bernard Madoff's investment scheme. While economics and statistics teach us how we *should* think about probability and outcomes when choosing between alternatives, we rarely follow these principles when actually making decisions. More often than not, we make choices under risk intuitively rather than deliberatively.

How We *Should*, versus *Do*, Think About Probability

When statisticians use the term *probability*, they have something very specific in mind: a long-run relative frequency. A simple example is a coin toss: If we flip a coin a large number of times, it will come up heads about half the time; hence, we say the odds of either outcome are 50-50. It is a precise number that one can determine mathematically. But it is unusual that one can assign such precise probabilities to uncertain events, particularly rare ones. While we might be able to define the event (e.g., a terrorist attack), it is difficult if not impossible to define the complete set of alternative possibilities necessary to compute precise odds. The perceptions we form about risk are thus more a cognitive cocktail of objective facts, subjective feelings, and emotions—a blend that often causes beliefs about risk to stray widely from those a statistician might prescribe.

Consider, for example, the case of insurers writing policies for the World Trade Center prior to the 9/11 attacks. While all knew that there was some risk that the buildings could be damaged by a terrorist attack, it was impossible at the time of Silverstein's purchase of the property to assign a precise probability to such an event. In the absence of estimates based on past data, the underwriters did the only thing they could: They relied on their subjective beliefs about the likelihood of a future attack that would damage or destroy property and assumed that it was highly unlikely.

While there are a number of reasons subjective beliefs about probability often stray from beliefs formulated by a statistician, psychologists have identified three main reasons: the *availability bias*, or the tendency to ground beliefs about risk in how easy it is to imagine bad outcomes; the *optimism bias*, or the tendency to believe that we are more immune than others to bad outcomes; and the *compounding bias*, or the tendency to underestimate cumulative risk.

The Curse of Intuition: The Availability Bias

In a 1980 airing of his late-night talk show, Johnny Carson made famous a mathematical problem involving computing probabilities called the birthday paradox, which works like this. Imagine a studio audience of 70 people where each is asked to announce the day and month in which he or she was born. "What are the chances that there is at least one pair of birthdays with the same date among the 70 people?" Intuition says that the odds of this happening are small. After all, it is rare to run into someone with the same birthday as ours. For this reason, many people would find it surprising that in an audience of 70, it is a virtual certainty that two will have the same birthday; the probability is 99.9%.[46]

Why does our intuition fail us in this case? The reason is that our minds instinctively lead us to try to solve the problem the same way that we estimate the odds of most things in life: By trying to imagine how often the event occurs based on our own experience. In the case of the birthday problem, an individual is likely to focus on the number of times he has met someone who was born on the same month and day as he. The likelihood of the person finding a match is very small, even with 70 people.[47] The birthday paradox, however, focuses on a different problem: the probability that *any* pair of individuals in a sample of 70 people has the same birthday.[48]

The tendency to estimate the likelihood of a specific event occurring on the basis of our own personal experience has been termed the *availability bias*, and it helps explain why we often have distorted perceptions of risk in a wide variety of settings.[49] With respect to the risk of terrorism, in the year prior to 9/11, insurers gave little thought to the possibility that terrorists could bring down both towers of the WTC, simply because such a catastrophic event would have been hard to imagine. It had been six years since any such major incident had occurred in the United States (the Oklahoma City bombing), the federal government had invested substantial resources in detecting and preventing repeats of such attacks, and it was hard to envision the possibility that two of the largest office buildings in the United States could collapse due to coordinated plane hijackings.

After the event occurred, the availability bias had the opposite effect of producing subjective beliefs that the risk of terrorism was much *higher* than actually plausible—a bias that had its own destructive effects. Insurers now perceived terrorism as a very salient risk and viewed another attack as extremely likely in the near future. As such, they concluded that it was an uninsurable risk. The few insurers who were willing to offer coverage were able to charge a very high premium because commercial enterprises were overly concerned about being protected. One firm, for example, paid $900,000 to protect itself against $9 million in damage to their facility from a terrorist attack in the coming year. If one calculates the implied odds of a terrorist attack damaging the building based on this insurance premium, it is 1 in 10 ($900,000 / $9 million), an estimate almost certainly much larger than the actual probability.

In a similar fashion, a large number of potential air travellers reacted to their newly elevated fears of terrorism by getting into their cars to reach destinations to which they would ordinarily have taken a plane. In 2002, for example, air passenger miles fell between 12% and 20%, while road use surged[50]—a change that Garrick Blalock and colleagues concluded resulted in the needless loss of 2,300 lives.[51]

What travellers overlooked at the time, of course, was that the risk of disaster while driving or riding in a car is much higher than that of flying, even given a perceived heightened risk of a terrorist attack overall. In the year after 9/11, though, images of planes flying into the World Trade Center would have been much easier to bring to mind than auto crashes on interstate highways—it is the salience of imagined events, not actuarial odds, that is key in driving behavior. The statistical data reveal that there is a 1 in 11 million chance that a person will be killed in a plane crash. If one compares the safety of planes relative to cars on a per-mile basis, the likelihood of being killed in a car is 720 times greater than that of flying.[52]

This psychic boomerang associated with the availability bias has been widely documented in other contexts, such as what causes people to buy insurance. Just prior to the 1989 Loma Prieta earthquake in California, only 22% of homeowners in the Bay Area had earthquake coverage. Although residents knew they were living in a seismically active region, it had been 83 years since a quake of magnitude 7 or higher hit the area—the great San Francisco earthquake took place in 1906, long before most were born. But the sudden realization that severe quakes *can* happen—the Loma Prieta registered 7.1 on the Richter scale—caused residents suddenly to elevate their subjective beliefs about the risk. Four years later, 36.6% of residents had purchased earthquake insurance—a 72% increase in coverage.[53] Similarly, the Northridge, California, earthquake of 1994 led to a significant demand for earthquake insurance. For example, more than two-thirds of the homeowners surveyed in nearby Cupertino County had purchased earthquake insurance in 1995.[54] There have been no severe earthquakes in California since Northridge, and only 10% of homeowners in seismic areas of the state have earthquake insurance today. If a severe quake hits the Bay Area or Los Angeles in the near future, the damage could be as high as $200 billion, and it is likely that most homeowners suffering damage will be financially unprotected.[55]

"It Will Not Happen to Me": The Optimism Bias

A related error arises when people form perceptions of risk: the tendency to believe that they are more immune than others to threats. This is the *optimism bias*. A classic study of this effect was published by Neil Weinstein in 1980.[56] He asked people to estimate the probability of uncertain future life events (such that one's marriage would end in divorce, one's car would be stolen, or one would be diagnosed with lung cancer) in one of two ways: the probability for the individual respondent and the probability for an average person in the population. In virtually all cases, people saw their own odds of escaping such misfortunes as being much higher than those of others; divorce, after all, is something that happens to other couples.

The optimism bias helps explain an apparent paradox that has surfaced in studies of how people prepare for natural hazards:

a tendency to concede that a hazard is likely to occur, but to take limited or no personal actions to reduce the potential damage. In a recent study, conducted by one of the authors,[57] on hurricane preparedness in advance of Hurricane Sandy, coastal residents in New Jersey believed forecasts that their community was about to be hit by a bad storm. In fact, they thought the storm would be more severe than it actually was. For example, some believed that there was more than an 80% chance their homes would experience sustained hurricane-force winds. In contrast, the National Hurricane Center's estimates of the probability of hurricane-force winds striking Atlantic City were never more than 32%. But here is the surprise: When asked what actions they were taking to prepare for the storm, most residents displayed a surprising laxness. Only slightly more than half of respondents who had removable storm shutters on their houses indicated that they were putting them up. Only 21% indicated that they had plans in place if they needed to evacuate.

The reason for this apparent disconnect became clear when residents were then asked to estimate the probability that their homes would suffer property damage as a result of the hurricane. Their estimates were less than half of those they gave when asked about the probability that they would experience damaging winds. In a nutshell, while residents believed that a hurricane was coming and that it would be bad, they also had faith that when it arrived they would personally escape harm.

There are two principal reasons for people being excessively optimistic that harm is something that happens to other people. One is the availability bias we've just discussed. Most of the time, harm *does* come to others, therefore instances in which one did *not* experience harm will come to mind much more readily than those in which one did. If a storm is approaching, one is more likely to think of damage in *other* places—floods in New Orleans, tornados in Oklahoma. It would be hard to imagine a storm surge from a hurricane inundating our home or strong winds detaching the roof if we have not experienced such a disaster before. The media play a key role in this regard by highlighting the damage that occurs in disasters with graphic photos of other people's misfortunes.

Yet this is only half the story. The second, and more serious, reason for people's excessive optimism is that we are also prone to construct scenarios that *we hope* will happen. We shut out images of our living room being underwater, of our homes' roofs being blown off. We would much prefer to think of the ways that we will escape harm rather than experience it. Psychologists term this effect *motivated reasoning*; that is, a tendency to selectively gather and process information that is most congruent with a desired goal or outcome.[58]

A tragic example of this behavior occurred during the great Labor Day Hurricane of 1935, when 257 World War I veterans lost their lives in the Florida Keys awaiting an escape train that never arrived. Knowing that the barracks the veterans were staying in would not be strong enough to survive a hurricane, officials ordered a train to be sent from Miami to evacuate them. A tragic mistake was made, however, in deciding *when* to send the train. The official in charge of the evacuation optimistically focused on how much time would be required to get to the Florida Keys and back under *normal* circumstances—not during a hurricane on Labor Day. He overlooked, for example, the fact that it would be difficult to quickly round up a crew on a holiday and that drawbridges would be open as boaters tried to move their vessels to safety. When the train finally made it to the Keys, it was too late; the storm's tidal surge had begun to submerge the tracks, and evacuation was impossible. At daybreak, it was discovered that most of the veterans in the camps had perished, along with more than 200 other Keys residents.

Underestimation of Cumulative Risk: The Compounding Bias

Another source of error arises when people perceive the risk of rare events: a tendency to focus on the low probability of an adverse event in the immediate future rather than on the relatively high probability over a longer time period. Consider again the case of the World Trade Center. On the eve of 9/11, the risk of a terrorist attack was probably the furthest thing from most people's minds for good reason: the odds of such a thing happening the next day was extraordinarily small. If someone had told investors, for example, that there was a 1-in-100 chance that a catastrophic terrorist attack would occur in any year during the lease of the WTC, they might have given this risk some consideration but still assumed it was not worth worrying about. But here's the rub: While a 1-in-100 chance of a disaster occurring in any one year is indeed quite small, extrapolated out over the life of a 99-year lease, that same risk becomes quite large. To be precise, there would be a 63% chance that a catastrophic attack would happen at least once in 100 years.[59] That *is* a risk that an investor would likely take more seriously.

This kind of oversight is commonplace in day-to-day life. If, one morning, we see an aged tree hanging over our house and are trying to decide whether to hire an arborist to prune it, we might well feel there is no urgency to the matter: The odds that the tree will fall *that day* are, after all, very small. But, of course, this is not the relevant calculation one should make. One should be thinking about the probability that the tree will fall *sometime in the foreseeable future*, and act on that likelihood.

There are two principal reasons that people are prone to underestimate long-term risk. First, when trying to compute compound probabilities, our brains tend to be overly influenced by short-term considerations, which come most easily to mind, an effect termed *anchoring bias*. To understand this, consider the problem of calculating the odds that a tree will fall on your house while you're living there over the course of several years. One quick way to do this would be to think of a probability you can be reasonably confident about, such as the probability that the tree will fall today, and then adjust that probability upward. This upward adjustment, however, is likely to be insufficient. Our initial estimate of the probability of the tree falling today, which is very small, will unduly *anchor* our estimate that it will probably fall over the course of several years.

Another reason for the focus on short-term risk is the way others present it to us. To illustrate, consider the case of flood insurance. In the United States, the Federal Emergency Management Agency (FEMA) operates the National Flood Insurance Program, which communicates flood risk to homeowners in terms of expected return periods. For example, a homeowner might be shown a map indicating that his residence lies in the "100-year floodplain," where a damaging flood might be expected once a century. Is this a high risk? We conjecture that most people would not see it that way; after all, time scales over decades are hard enough to grasp mentally, much less over a century. The tendency to ignore this risk might be exacerbated if the location recently experienced an actual flood. In that case, the "once-in-a-century" reference might wrongly be construed as implying that the home is safe for another 99 years. Yet note that if the National Flood Insurance Program told homeowners that, over the course of a 25-year period, the chances of at least one flood occurring was greater than one in five (that is, the same risk as once in a century, but conveyed in a mentally more manageable way),[60] the homeowners might suddenly be far more concerned, and see flood insurance as worth purchasing.

Recap: The Bane of Optimism

One of the major challenges of preparing for catastrophic events is that, unlike with flipping a coin or playing roulette, we cannot assign precise probabilities to potential disasters. When Larry Silverstein, the banks, and insurers were poised to support the purchase of the World Trade Center in July 2001, there were no actuarial tables that listed the probability of a terrorist attack, nor even good statistical models from which they could have derived reliable estimates. Nor do these exist today. While we usually cannot assign precise probabilities to rare events, good decisions can still be made if our subjective estimates are well calibrated—that is, if our estimates, while sometimes being too high and sometimes too low, on average tend to converge to their objective values.

The key lesson of this chapter is that our perception of the likelihood of rare adverse events will often stray widely from objective risk levels due to a blend of three biases: the *availability bias*, the tendency to equate the likelihood of an event with its salience and the ease with which it can be imagined; the *optimism bias*, the tendency to believe we are more immune than others to adverse events and thus to treat the risk as below our threshold level of concern; and the *compounding bias*, the tendency to focus on the low probability of an adverse event happening in the immediate future rather than on the relatively high probability of its occurring over a longer time period. When taken together, these three systematic biases can lead to the kind of misjudgments illustrated in this chapter: a mistaken belief that that the risk of catastrophe is too low to worry about or, if it does occur, that we will be immune from its worst effects.

Before we move on, we might note that all the biases we have talked about so far (myopia, amnesia, and optimism) might be overcome if we had effective heuristics, or rules of thumb, for investing in protection—that is, rules that required us to mentally assess the costs and benefits of obtaining that protection. Indeed, often when we are faced with choices about preparedness, this is what happens: We use heuristics that make selective use of the information available to us. Over the next three chapters we will explore the nature of the systematic biases associated with choice and their impact on decision making under conditions of risk and uncertainty.

Chapter 5

The Inertia Bias

In September 2004, the city of New Orleans had a problem. Hurricane Ivan, packing 140 mph winds, was spinning northward through the Gulf of Mexico, with computer models predicting a direct hit on New Orleans in three days. Although the city is one of the most frequent targets for hurricane hits in the United States, officials knew it was underprepared for a storm of this magnitude. The city lacked the transportation infrastructure to evacuate some 100,000 residents who either did not have cars or were too frail to move, and it did not have the facilities to provide alternative shelter. As the storm bore down, officials suggested that the Superdome serve as a shelter of last resort, but the facility's managers cautioned against this.[61] The Superdome had nowhere near the resources needed to house thousands of residents for an extended period, and even if it did, the city lacked the transportation infrastructure that would be needed to ferry residents from their flooded homes to the facility.

The doomsday scenario, however, never materialized. Two days later, Ivan changed course, weakened, and eventually made landfall on the Alabama-Florida border, leaving New Orleans largely unscathed. City officials and residents breathed a sigh of relief, but also realized that Ivan had exposed a number of preparedness weaknesses that needed fixing. The problem was how to do it on a limited budget. There was the evacuation problem, the traffic flow problem, and the shelter problem. There was also the issue of an aging levee and pump system, the two essential lines of protection in the face of a storm. It was hard to know where to start. But there was at least one bit of good news: The next hurricane season was a full eight months away, leaving officials plenty of time at least to get a start on the most pressing problems.

Yet, in the end, little was done. The following August, Hurricane Katrina made landfall on the Mississippi Gulf coast just east of the city, killing more than 1,500 people and producing more than $100 billion in damages—the costliest hurricane in US history. When Katrina hit, New Orleans's aged (and incomplete) levee system was breached in 55 places, and floods gradually filled the city like a soup bowl. Thousands who were unable to evacuate sought refuge in the Superdome, but just as the city had been warned a year earlier, the arena proved inadequate as a shelter. The result was a humanitarian disaster that had few precedents in American history. And while billions in federal aid eventually allowed New Orleans to get back on its feet, the storm left scars that took years to recover from. Of the 400,000 residents displaced by the storm, 140,000, or 29% of the city's pre-storm population, have never returned.[62]

What went wrong during Katrina? One might be tempted to point a finger at the perceptual biases that we discuss in the previous three chapters—myopia, amnesia, and unwarranted optimism, and indeed each of these contributed to the lack of preparedness in New Orleans to some extent. But we suggest that to fully understand what happened with Katrina, one needs to look to a different kind of bias, that which arises when people (and organizations) are faced both with difficult choices under risk and uncertainty and with conflicting goals: the inertial tendency to do nothing. In early 2005, emergency officials were under no illusions about the risks New Orleans faced, but the multitude of challenges and competing interests presented no clear or easy path forward. In the fog of this deliberation, the city did what we all often do when we are unsure how to proceed: It made no choice at all.

Default Options and the Lure of the Status Quo

The tendency to look for, and choose, default courses of actions is one of the most robust biases in decision making. One of the first such demonstrations was provided in 1993 by one of the authors and his colleagues, who studied the effects of a difference in how auto insurance contracts were written in two adjoining states, Pennsylvania and New Jersey.[63] Both states offered car owners the opportunity to buy either lower-priced policies that came with a limited right to sue in the case of an accident or a higher-priced policy that had no such restriction. The two states differed with respect to their default options. In New Jersey, the default was the plan with the limited right to sue, while in Pennsylvania, the opposite held: If car owners did not respond, they maintained their current insurance contract. In other words, the default option was the status quo. The researchers found that this simple policy difference had a huge effect on policy preferences; in Pennsylvania, only 30% of drivers opted to restrict their right to sue, while in New Jersey, where such an option was the default, 79% maintained the status quo. Similar results were obtained in a hypothetical study of how 136 university employees would respond to these policy differences. The effect was even larger in the real world than in the controlled experiment.

The explanation seems simple enough. Accidents and insurance contracts are not things that people particularly want to think about. Hence, in such situations, there is a natural tendency to look for a way out, a way not to make a decision. Defaults provide an easy mental exit, a way, in essence, in which one can make a choice without making one. Examples of the powerful effects of defaults abound. For example, in a 2003 study of organ donation preferences in Europe, Eric Johnson and Dan Goldstein found that the percentage of drivers whose licenses listed them as an organ donor varied enormously across countries—a difference driven almost completely by whether the default was to opt in to being a donor or to opt out.[64]

The Psychology of Defaults

In many aspects of life, a tendency to look for a default option is a useful, intuitive (System 1), tie-breaking heuristic, a mental hack that prevents our System 2 getting us too mired in inconsequential deliberations. If we are unsure whether to order the Caesar or the Cobb salad for lunch, or whether to pick the Snickers or the Milky Way from the vending machine, it probably doesn't matter which option we choose—each, in the end, will give us similar amounts of pleasure. Because it is a waste of System 2 resources to spend too much time deliberating over it, our brains instinctively hand the problem off to System 1 intuitions that look for quick-and-easy tie breakers. Defaults serve that role: You order the salad you ate yesterday. You choose the snack you spot first. It is an easy and efficient way of making a choice.

The problem, of course, is that such heuristics can be dangerous when evoked in contexts in which the stakes are high. Decisions to take protective action are a case in point. Investments in protective action almost never arise by default; one needs to write a check to secure insurance, pay for a safer home, make the effort to evacuate. In addition, if one considers investing in a protective measure, one needs to spend time and energy examining alternative options. How much insurance coverage does one want, and is it worth taking a higher deductible to reduce one's premium? Should you invest money in flood proofing your house or elevating it, and how expensive will these measures be? The more our System 2 spins its wheels addressing these questions or determining whether investments should be made now or considered at a later time, the more likely we will turn the wheel over to our System 1 instincts to maintain the status quo as the default option—which, in cases of undertaking protection measures, normally means doing nothing.

Of course, there will be times when the default is to take some type of action, and this can be no less dangerous. Bad habits are hard to break because our brains keep defaulting to them; smokers need to muster all their System 2 energies to overcome the urge to light up after a meal; dieters have a hard time breaking the instinct to forage for snacks late at night. Or consider the case of the fight-or-flight instincts that arise when we are exposed to an immediate threat—a System 1 impulse to take action that can be hard to shut down when it is triggered. It is, presumably, just this instinct that contributed to the tragedies of the Moore family and Air France 447 that we discussed in chapter 1. In both cases, of course, doing nothing was the safer path. Yet those decisions to *avoid* taking action would have demanded the greater power of reason—for Glenda Moore to understand that it would be safer to stay at home during Hurricane Sandy, and for the copilot to understand that pointing the nose of the plane up risked a stall.

When Choosing Defaults Can Be Thoughtful

Up to this point we have portrayed the tendency to choose naïve defaults as a System 1 bias, an instinctive response to uncertainty for which we often have little conscious awareness. Yet clearly this is not always the case. One assumes, for example, that more than primitive instinct was at work when the city of New Orleans chose to take limited corrective actions after Hurricane Ivan's near miss. Here city officials had plenty of information at hand about the risks, and very likely deliberated over possible actions (or nonactions) in budget and planning meanings. Yet the result was much the same: Indecision over what actions to take led to no decision.

To explain *thoughtful* preferences for defaults, we need to turn to a different psychological mechanism, that of loss aversion. In the late 1970s, psychologists Daniel Kahneman and Amos Tversky accumulated a large body of evidence showing that human judgments tend to be marked by two features:

1. A tendency to value things relative to a reference point, which often is the status quo; and

2. A tendency to see a negative change from the reference point (losses) as being much more painful than an identical positive change (gains).[65]

Hence the well-known example of how we feel at the end of a night of gambling at a casino: The discomfort of having lost $100 is much greater than the pleasure of having won $100. This effect is a deeply engrained feature of how we value things whether we are making decisions intuitively using System 1 behavior or, more deliberatively, by engaging in a more systematic System 2 decision making process.

Loss aversion helps explain how preferences for defaults can emerge from otherwise thoughtful deliberations over options. Consider, for example, a hypothetical city's decision whether to fund a much-needed levee repair. A budget committee meeting on the topic would likely, and sensibly, discuss the pros and cons of the investment, on the positive side. For example, advocates would point to the reduction of flood risk and, possibly, to the new employment the project would generate. Yet there would also be discussion of the downsides to incurring these costs. Some might note that the money could be better spent on a project to elevate homes in flood areas, or the investment might prove insufficient given a truly severe storm. Loss aversion prescribes that in such discussions, the weight of the cons will exceed those of the pros, leading to a bias against investing. What exacerbates this bias is that the funds for these new projects invariably compete with existing projects where continued investment is the default, such as for the completion of a sports facility. Here the tables are turned; the pros are freeing up money that might better be used for a levee repair, but there also exist cons, such as public anger over delay in the completion of the stadium. In this battle, the default decision to continue funding existing projects usually wins out.

The Malleability of Defaults

This brings us to one final question: Might it be possible to *alter* defaults so that they favor safer actions? What makes this problem challenging is that, by definition, defaults are "ghost alternatives" in a choice problem—that is, options that people revert to in an effort to *avoid* making a choice. People or organizations who opt to do nothing when faced with uncertainty about how best to invest in protection typically do not see themselves as having made an active decision to remain passive; in their minds, they have simply put the decision "on hold" for a bit. Likewise, people who follow the instinct to flee when faced with a storm threat may not be aware that they have, in effect, made an implicit decision not to shelter in place. Of course, both decisions have consequences that are just as real as would have been the case had the choices been explicit. This thus creates a logical quandary when it comes to encouraging safer actions: How can we steer people to make better decisions when they are unware that they are making decisions in the first place?

To help address this, research on preferences for defaults and status quo biases has found that defaults are, in fact, often quite malleable.[66] For example, consider the finding just noted that there was a large difference between New Jersey and Pennsylvania residents in their preferences for full or limited tort insurance policies, a difference that depended on whether one had to opt in or opt out. A likely explanation is that residents assumed that the current insurance policy had been determined by experts to be the best for most people in the state when, in fact, no such studies had been undertaken. To the degree that people hold this generous view when it comes to government, then altering people's behavior by changing defaults might prove surprisingly easy: People would view having to opt *out* of something as the *right* move, the one recommended by a benevolent government wishing to spare the population the need to make what might otherwise be a difficult choice.

In other cases, defaults are the option invoked by the application of a naïve tie-breaking heuristic: the option being preferred by the majority, or the one closest at hand. In a 1988 study of how young university professors (presumably an intelligent lot) allocated their retirement portfolio between stocks and bonds, economists William Samuelson and Richard Zeckhauser found that the modal allocation was 50-50, an overly conservative mix that few investment advisers would recommend.[67] Yet this preference is easy to explain. Participants in the study agreed that an optimal portfolio should include a mix of stocks and bonds, but there was considerable uncertainty as to how much to allocate to each one. Rather than devoting time to examining this question through a more systematic analysis of the financial impact of various allocations over time, the professors hedged their bets by deciding to allocate half their funds to stocks and the other half to bonds—an easy and comfortable choice that could be defended given the uncertainty associated with future returns. To the degree that there may be similar well-known choice heuristics in other contexts, it might be possible to anticipate the kind of decision-making mistakes people will make and, in turn, use this knowledge to preclude those mistakes.

Recap: The Bane of Cognitive Inertia

The main message of this chapter is that one of the major reasons we often err when making protective decisions is that we usually prefer not to make such decisions at all. We tend to be highly inertial in our thinking, preferring to stay with the status quo rather than follow new paths of action, and to look for defaults that free us from the labors of difficult, deliberative (System 2) thinking. Like all the biases we have discussed in this book, inertia as a survival tool is a double-edged sword: It is of enormous benefit with regard to energy conservation, one that allows us to operate, most of the time, on autopilot, thus allowing our System 2 powers of deliberative thinking to be well rested when they need to invoked.

Yet, on the downside, it is an instinct not easily turned off when first invoked: When we *should* be thinking carefully about what to do, inertia provides us an all-too-easy escape hatch, one that leads to passivity when action is called for and action when passivity is called for.

Preferences for defaults, however, is not the only bias that can get us into trouble. Our brains like to take shortcuts, and when we *do* employ them, they can cause us to make imperfect decisions based on only a subset of information available to us.

In the next chapter, we take up the problem of decision simplification.

Chapter 6

The Simplification Bias

On Saturday, May 23, 2015, near a stop sign on Sixtieth and Fairmont in Milwaukee, a motorcycle struck a car and both the motorcyclist and his passenger were ejected from their bike. The motorcyclist and the driver of the car both suffered minor, nonthreatening injuries, but the motorcyclist's passenger suffered a serious head injury and died. The motorcyclist was wearing a helmet, but his passenger was not. This difference was widely credited with saving the former's life. Two weeks later, a 23-year-old man from nearby Racine was riding his motorcycle near the intersection of Highways 31 and 38 in Mount Pleasant, 40 miles away from Milwaukee, when the bike ricocheted off one car and collided with another. The motorcyclist was not wearing a helmet and died at the scene of the accident.

For many of us it is hard to understand why someone would choose not to wear a helmet when riding a motorcycle. Helmets are inexpensive, and easy to wear and store, and the evidence of their safety value is unambiguous. According to the National Highway Traffic Safety Administration, for example, helmet wearing is credited with saving the lives of 1,669 motorcyclists in 2014, reducing motorcycle fatalities by 27%.[68] Likewise, a 2009 study by Martin Croce and colleagues at the University of Tennessee of almost 2 million motorcyclists who were admitted to hospitals found similar evidence that wearing helmets significantly reduces the risk of brain and spinal injuries.[69] To illustrate the magnitude of these costs, in 2014 a hospital study of 192 injured motorcyclists in Michigan calculated that medical expenses for injured helmetless riders was $11,400 (or 53%) higher than for helmeted riders.[70] Despite the overwhelming evidence documenting the benefits of helmets, today only 19 states have laws that require all motorcyclists to wear them, and even in states where helmet wearing is mandatory, the law is often violated.[71]

Thresholds and Single-Cue Choice Policies

There is, of course, a simple explanation for why some motorcyclists refuse to wear helmets: They have thought about the matter and have decided that the personal costs of using a helmet exceed the benefits. Wearing a helmet, after all, has its downsides: One *does* have to go through the effort to put one on, and helmets are typically built for safety rather than style. Perhaps even more important, motorcyclists might see helmets as contrary to the common ethos of autonomy inherent in riding a motorcycle with the great feeling that comes from having the wind blow through your hair. After all, James Dean never wore one. While one could quarrel with such values, theirs could simply be a mental calculation that differs from ours.

We suggest, however, that other factors play a more important role in this decision. When getting on a motorcycle without a helmet, drivers and passengers are not just underweighing the risks of having an accident; they are not even considering this possibility at all. It is below their threshold level of concern. While a motorcyclist might have every intention of undertaking a deliberative (System 2) assessment of the many pros and cons of wearing a helmet before getting on a bike, this is a cognitively difficult process. There are too many factors to consider, too little knowledge about them, and too little time to do the mental math. Our brains thus look for an easy way out: a System 1 solution. While one such route is to look for a default as discussed in the previous chapter, here we suggest that another factor is at play: the tendency to make the choice by considering only the small set of factors that come most readily to mind. Given that the risk of an accident is small, this would likely be discarded as a decision factor of relevance. For motorcyclists who don't wear helmets, the greater risk of brain injury from not wearing one never makes it onto their cognitive radar screen.

Evidence that people often ignore probability information when making decisions under uncertainty is widespread. A 1997 study by Oswald Huber and colleagues, for example, found that when evaluating several risky managerial decisions, only 22% of managers sought out information on the likelihood of adverse events occurring.[72] Even when another group of respondents was given precise probability information, less than 20% mentioned this attribute in their verbal protocols on factors that influenced their decisions. Similarly, in a 1995 study of how people decide whether to purchase warranties for items such as stereos, computers, and VCRs, one of the authors discovered that buyers rarely list the probability that the product needs repair as an influential factor.[73]

What causes this cognitive oversight? It is important to emphasize that the fact that probabilities of disasters are typically small is not the reason per se that those probabilities are overlooked. One of the most robust findings regarding decisions made under risk is that when small probabilities are made explicit and emphasized to us—for example, we are told that a given surgical procedure has 1-in-10,000 chance of producing deadly side effects—we actually tend to mentally *inflate* the influence of this number, not underweigh it.[74] The reason is that our minds have a hard time dealing with very small probabilities, hence we tend to mentally group them in simple categories: For example, an event has no chance of occurring, has a small chance, or is likely. As a result, our minds see a huge difference in *no* chance of something bad occurring versus *some* chance—no matter how small that chance. Behavioral economists call this the *certainty premium*. Although a 1-in-10,000 chance of a deadly side effect occurring is objectively quite small, it would be seen as large when compared to a treatment for which there was *no* risk of a side effect. To illustrate this effect, experiments show that people are willing to pay far more to have the probability of a severe risk (such as dying) reduced from .0001 to 0 than from .0002 to .0001—even though the mathematical benefit is obviously the same.

Yet, as we have repeatedly noted, it is rare in life that we ever encounter precise probabilities like this, particularly for disasters, and it is the inherent *vagueness* of small probabilities, not the numbers themselves, that cause us to discard those probabilities as a cue when making decisions. When a motorcyclist gets on her bike, she can hear the engine, feel the handle bars and seat, and experience the breeze. But the concept of the probability of a crash is an ephemeral quantity, a cue that's out there, but one whose value and meaning are vague at best. Because our minds, by nature, are drawn to that which is salient, probabilities are a consideration that often gets left in the dust.

The Single-Action Bias

The tendency to make decisions based on the consideration of only a small subset of cues can have harmful effects on preparedness that go beyond ignoring probability information. One simplification is termed the single-action bias: When faced with a hazard for which multiple preparedness actions are required, decision makers generally feel that their needs have been met after undertaking a small subset of actions—perhaps only one or two.[75] As an example, consider the problem of retrofitting a home to make it more resilient to windstorm hazards. What makes such retrofits challenging is that mitigation requires multiple integrated steps, and the quality of an investment is only as good as the weakest link. Putting on more wind-resistant shingles is of little help if the home has gables that have not also been reinforced.[76] Given a limited budget, a homeowner might thus (reasonably) decide to make the improvements in steps, but stop after the first one, feeling that he has taken sufficient action on this concern that resources can now be diverted to other household needs.

The single-action bias has several psychological origins. One is cognitive dissonance: When a problem arises, we feel an elevated sense of dissonance, and search for a way to reduce it by taking remedial action. But once an action has been undertaken, dissonance is reduced, making it hard to motivate us to take additional actions. Consider the case of responses to hurricane threats. If a hurricane warning is issued for a city, residents will likely feel a strong urge to take some protective action, and there will be no shortage of advice from the media. People would likely be urged to secure extra food, water for three days, extra batteries, and so on.[77] Yet once the first action is taken, say, extra food secured, there will be a natural tendency for our brains to see the problem as having been solved. This reduced sense of dissonance then acts to suppress the sense of urgency to take additional actions. A good example of this arose in one of the author's studies of preparation in advance of two hurricanes in 2012, Isaac and Sandy.[78] In both cases the vast majority of threatened residents (more than 80%) indicated undertaking some type of protective action; they were well informed about the threat, and recognized the need to respond to it, but when they were asked to elaborate on their preparations, these turned out to be surprisingly limited in scope, such as buying extra food and filling the car's tank with gas. Disturbingly missing were measures that would have been essential had the storm impact proven to be severe, such as making plans for where to go should an evacuation be necessary.

Another psychological origin for the single-action bias is the procrastination bias we discussed in chapter 2. An inherent feature of virtually all protective actions is that they involve up-front costs and delayed benefits. When a hurricane is approaching, one has to lay out money to buy stocks of water that may or may not be needed in two days' time. When retrofitting a roof, one has to pay now for a series of improvements whose benefits could lie years in the future, if at all. As we discussed in chapter 2, each of these actions is psychologically difficult, and becomes ever more so when *a series* of actions is required to achieve adequate protection. The first one or two steps might be undertaken, but the others left for tomorrow. Residents may have every intention of developing an evacuation plan and buying a generator, but more pressing immediate needs push these actions to the psychic backburner.

Recap: The Problem of Decision Simplification

The moral of this chapter is not a particularly happy one: If our goal is to encourage people to improve the protective decisions they make, simply encouraging them to avoid instinct (System 1 thinking) and engage in deliberative thinking (System 2) will probably not get the job done. The reason is that even when we *do* try to reason through problems, our cognitive calculus tends to be simplified. As an example, our brains tend to process only those cues it perceives as being large and thus meriting attention—which is a particular problem for extreme events whose probability of occurring is, by definition, quite small (though with large consequences when the events occur). Worse yet, when a large number of cues grab our attention, we typically lack the mental capacity to process all of them comprehensively, so we look for shortcuts, such as making the decision based on only the most salient of the cues, ignoring all the others (even when they carry important implications for our safety). Finally, because decisions about protection are but a small subset of the full array of problems we face on a given day, we tend to allocate to them only a small set of mental airtime—meaning that protective investments are often incomplete (the single-action bias).

Yet there may be a way out of this apparent quandary. While it may well be that, as individuals, we lack the ability to make good decisions, we might be able to overcome this by looking for wisdom in the crowd—that is, by imitating the (hopefully better) decisions made by others. This possibility will be the focus of our next chapter.

Chapter 7

The Herding Bias

Few 1970s television and nightclub personalities were bigger than John Davidson. His combination of youth, good looks, and calming music style was just what the doctor ordered for a generation of Americans seeking an alternative to the counterculture rock stars preferred by many baby boomers of the 1960s. It was thus quite a coup when, in May 1977, the Beverly Hills Supper Club in Southgate, Kentucky (a Cincinnati, Ohio, bedroom community), managed to book him for a performance. Tickets went quickly, and the club rushed to squeeze extra tables in the venue to accommodate the demand.

The night started routinely enough. Guests crowded into the club's Cabaret Room, took their seats at their tables, and enjoyed the performance of two comedians who were warm-ups for Davidson's act. As the warm-up act was finishing, however, members of the staff noticed something that was far from routine: A fire had erupted in an adjoining room. They first tried to handle the matter themselves, using small fire extinguishers. But it quickly became clear that this was far from sufficient, and the fire soon raged out of control. While management was preoccupied with trying to extinguish the growing blaze, an 18-year-old busboy took it upon himself to take the stage and inform the patrons that a fire had broken out nearby. He urged everyone to leave, at least until the situation could be brought back under control.

While many in the audience heeded his advice, others hesitated, unsure what to do. They had paid a handsome price for the tickets, and this was an evening they had been anticipating for a long time. Furthermore, the advice to flee was coming from a young busboy, not a fire marshal. The young man suggested different ways of leaving, but did not clarify which path was the best one to take. Given this uncertainty, the audience did what many of us would have done: They looked to see what others were doing, as if *they* might have greater insight into the situation. It was only when the main room's lights went out that a mass rush for the doors began, but by then the combination of smoke and confusion made escape for many impossible. By the time the smoke had cleared, 165 people were dead.

In the weeks that followed the fire, survivors and the press angrily pointed the finger of blame on the club's management, and for good reason. The club was grossly overcrowded, with almost 1,000 people jammed in a room meant for at most 600. The facility had no smoke alarm or sprinkler system and not enough exits for the number of patrons it had admitted. The building was made of highly combustible materials and what proved to be the trigger of the fire was a faulty electrical system. In the end, the club had no emergency protocol for evacuating the building should an event like this occur.

In some ways, the tragedy of the Beverly Hills Supper Club was the result of almost all the biases that we have discussed thus far: indecision and misplaced optimism by patrons, myopia by managers, and the default option to stay. However, to understand the disaster fully, we need to consider an additional bias that plagues our decisions under risk: the instinct to follow herds.

When patrons first heard the busboy say the word *fire*, it may well have triggered a System 1 instinct to flee the room—an instinct that had great survival value if one heeded it immediately. But this instinct had to compete with another, equally strong response to danger: that of staying with the group. As precious seconds ticked away, many hesitated, loath to break from the apparent safety of their companions, looking to others for guidance that would not be forthcoming. These moments of hesitation proved fatal.

The instinct to look for wisdom in crowds also helps explain the club's earlier failure to invest in protective measures. Given uncertainty about how to trade off the benefits of a smoke alarm and sprinkler system against their considerable cost, it would have been natural for management to look to the decisions that other clubs had made. In the 1970s the city of Southgate had no laws requiring businesses to have fire control systems, and as a result, few had them. The owners of the Beverly Hills Supper Club could rationalize not having fire safety measures by indicating that they were just behaving the same way that other clubs were. The absence of regulations or voluntarily adoption of fire control systems by others might also have been taken as evidence that the risk of fire must be small: If it were larger, surely there would be laws or regulations requiring protective measures.

The Double-Edged Sword of Social Norms

Like many of the biases we have discussed, the instinct to follow a herd is, more often than not, a good one. When faced with an outside threat, the old adage that there is safety in numbers is often quite valid: Two typically beats one. Likewise, when individual members of a social community become immunized against an infectious disease, this immunity has positive spillover effects by decelerating the spread of the disease within the entire group.[79] Likewise, the decline we have seen in individual rates of smoking in recent decades in the United States is due, in large part, to the development and acceptance of social norms against smoking.[80]

Where the instinct to follow the herd goes awry, however, is when it used in an information vacuum—when, in fact, the collective crowd is no better informed than the least informed of its individual members. In such cases, blind instincts to follow herds can have deleterious effects. Because the primary motivation for individual action is simply the presence of other individuals, a destructive social cascade, once started, can be hard to stop.

Consider, for example, the decision to purchase disaster insurance. While this decision rationally should be driven by a trade-off between risk exposure and cost, social norms often emerge as the greater driver. For example, a 2013 study of the factors that caused Queenslanders to buy flood insurance found that ownership was unrelated to perceptions of the probability of floods, but highly correlated with whether residents believed there was a social norm for the insurance.[81] Likewise, a 2012 study of Philippine villagers' decisions to buy micro insurance policies against typhoon risks similarly found that the major driver was whether a neighbor had such a policy.[82] In an earlier study of protection against flood and earthquake risk, one of the authors found that the most important factors determining whether a homeowner purchased earthquake or flood insurance was discussions with friends and neighbors rather than the perceived likelihood and consequences of a future disaster occurring.[83]

While herd behavior can lead to insufficient protection, it can also produce the opposite error, excessive investment in protection. A case in point is the swine flu panic of 2009. In early April of that year, a five-year-old boy in La Gloria, Mexico, became ill with flulike symptoms. Local villagers were quick to point a finger at its likely source: airborne germs being spread from a large pig farm in a neighboring village. There was nothing unique about the boy's illness that made the pigs particularly culpable; there was simply a widespread (and scientifically unfounded) belief that pigs were unhealthy, and thus were a convenient target of blame. Fortunately, the boy soon recovered, and swabs of the flu strain were sent off to Canada for testing.

The results of the testing surprised authorities at the World Health Organization (WHO). Rather than being a familiar strain, this seemed to be new one, a variation of the influenza virus of 1918 that was estimated to have killed between 50 and 100 million people around the world, mostly the very old and very young. Yet whether this variant had that potency was uncertain. Evidence from Mexico, for example, indicated that the virus was milder than the 1918 version, and was not differentially harmful to the old and young (the primary source of deaths in 1918). Nevertheless, the flu was spreading, and the WHO had to make a decision about what actions to take against this new strain, one that now had a popular (if unfounded) name: the swine flu.

In June 2009 the WHO issued a stage-six health alert for the disease, officially declaring it a pandemic. Throughout the world the word *pandemic* was all that public officials needed to hear. The government of Egypt ordered the slaughter of the country's entire livestock of pigs (the fact that the flu was not transmitted by pigs being immaterial), and in the United States, President Barack Obama declared swine flu a national emergency. Governments across the globe rushed to the doors of pharmaceutical companies with massive orders for preventive vaccines. But as the winter of 2009 turned to the spring of 2010, it became clear that the global hysteria was largely unfounded. Stocks of vaccine went unused, and in fact, rumors began to spread that the vaccine may have been more dangerous than the disease itself, causing narcolepsy in some children.[84] While this association was later discredited,[85] in many ways the harm had already been done, as it gave birth to a fear of vaccines among many that may prove deadly if a true pandemic emerges.

Similar behavior has been observed with respect to protection against whooping cough (pertussis) in the United Kingdom. The diphtheria-tetanus-pertussis (DTP) combination vaccine had been routinely used for more than 20 years, so that whooping cough had become a much less common disease in comparison with its incidence in the mid-20th century. In January 1974, however, an article described 36 children who were claimed to have suffered severe neurological complications following their DTP immunization. It reported that the vaccine was only marginally effective, and questioned whether its expected benefits outweighed its risks.Television documentaries and newspaper reports dramatized tragic stories of profoundly intellectually disabled children allegedly injured by the vaccine. Parents convinced that their children's disabilities had resulted from the pertussis immunization joined together to form an advocacy group, Parents of Vaccine-Damaged Children, which played a major role in focusing public attention on the issue.[86]

The result of all this negative publicity was a rapid fall in immunization rates against whooping cough. Vaccine uptake in the United Kingdom decreased from 81% to 31%, and pertussis epidemics followed, leading to the deaths of some children. Mainstream medical opinion continued to support the effectiveness and safety of the vaccine; public confidence was restored after the publication of a national reassessment of vaccine efficacy. Vaccine uptake then increased to levels above 90%, and disease incidence declined dramatically.[87]

The United States largely avoided controversy over the vaccine until a 1982 documentary, *DPT: Vaccine Roulette*, ignited a major wave of negative publicity. Angry parents formed vaccine victim advocacy groups analogous to those in Britain and enlisted the help of like-minded physicians. The controversy was fueled in 1985 by a book with the provocative title *A Shot in the Dark*, which highlights the possibility of severe brain damage from the pertussis vaccine.[88] Overall, the US medical profession remained strongly supportive of continuing the DTP vaccine, there was far less debate in the pages of medical journals than was the case in the United Kingdom, and immunization rates never fell significantly. Instead, the chief consequence of the US controversy was a dramatic rise in litigation that soon threatened the nation's vaccine supply. A series of congressional hearings culminated in the passage of the National

Childhood Vaccine Injury Compensation Act of 1986, which set up a no-fault compensation program for probable vaccine injuries.[89]

Today whooping cough, a highly contagious respiratory infection, still remains a public health priority despite the availability of vaccines for 70 years. According to 2008 estimates, pertussis caused 195,000 deaths in children younger than 5 years old worldwide, despite a global 82% vaccine coverage. While this burden remains overwhelmingly concentrated in developing countries, pertussis has also reemerged in some developed countries that maintain high vaccine coverage, such as the United States.[90] One of the reasons for this high outbreak is the fear that the vaccine will cause permanent brain damage or death, so that some parents refuse to give it to their babies.

The Polarization Effect, Opinion Leadership, and Fighting the Herd

The examples just given suggest that the link between instincts to follow herds and protective behavior is not a simple one: Sometimes it produces excessive risk taking, sometime excessive risk aversion. There is, however, a systematic pattern to these findings: By and large, group decisions tend to go the way of individual inclinations, but be more extreme—a result psychologists term the *group polarization* effect.[91] For example, the swine flu hysteria took hold because it amplified a natural fear people have of pandemics and contracting a disease. Similar behavior occurred in the United Kingdom with respect to the concerns about the safety of the pertussis vaccine in the 1970s, and it took well-designed controlled studies to alleviate these concerns. In cases where the individual feels it is unnecessary to undertake protection, such as purchasing flood insurance, friends and neighbors are likely to reinforce this decision and create a herd effect.

This same polarization effect influences the effectiveness of opinion leaders who try to lead herds. Leaders can amplify the collective decisions of the group and perhaps convince others to follow suit, but it would be a challenge for them to cause individuals to *change* their preexisting inclinations. To illustrate this, in 2008 the authors conducted a laboratory study of social leadership effects in earthquake mitigation.[92] In the study, participants were told that they would be living in an area prone to periodic earthquakes, and that they could purchase structural improvements to their homes that potentially mitigated the effects of quakes should one arise. At the end of the simulation, they would be paid an amount that was tied to the difference between their home value and the cost of mitigation if they undertook protective measures plus the cost of repairs from earthquakes that damaged their houses.

Throughout the simulation, they could observe the investment decisions made by others in their virtual community, and the damage they suffered from quakes. The key source of uncertainty in the simulation was whether the mitigation was cost effective; half the participants were placed in a world where mitigation was not cost-effective (hence the optimal investment was 0%), and the other half were placed in a world where mitigation was long-term effective (hence the optimal investment was 100%). Our interest was in observing whether communities could discover the optimal level of mitigation over repeated plays of the game. Few individuals in any of the communities discovered the optimal behavior. Rather, there was a social norm effect: The major driver of individual decisions about how much to invest was the average level of investment made by neighbors—50%.

We then sought to test whether this herd effect could be overcome by informing one player in each community of the true effectiveness of the mitigation measure to see whether he might emerge as an opinion leader. Other players knew that one among them had this information. That person's identity was not revealed, but could likely be inferred by observing players' investment behavior. For example, a player who was told that investments are ineffective would, presumably, invest 0% from the start. Did this "knowledge seeding" help communities learn? It did, but (quite surprisingly) only in the case where the right thing to do was *not* invest, the preferences that most individuals had at the start of the simulation. In these communities, players seemed to immediately recognize the informed player (who was not investing), and after two rounds of the game, almost all investments in mitigation had vanished, as they should have.

In contrast, in communities where mitigation was effective, rather than seeing investments increase over time, we saw them actually *decrease*. While players who were told that mitigation was effective invested more at the start of the simulation, this behavior was immediately imitated by others. Players acted as if they were looking for evidence to support their prior preference *not* to invest. Then, bizarrely, the informed players, seeing that their actions were not being followed, reduced their own investments. After multiple plays of the game, few players were making any investments at all, even though it was optimal for them to do so in the long run.

Recap: Is There Wisdom in Crowds?

In this chapter, we explored what some might see as a natural work-around for the individual decision biases we discussed in earlier chapters: The possibility that while individual decisions may be flawed, these flaws will be attenuated when the decisions are made in groups, where people can imitate the best decisions of others. Unfortunately, the key lesson of the chapter is that, at least when it comes to protective investments, that tends not to be the case: There is, as it turns out, little wisdom in crowds. People indeed have a strong instinct to look to the behavior of others as a source of guidance, but doing so often seems to intensify individual decision biases more than mollify them.

The reason for this failure is straightforward: When looking for people to imitate, we tend to focus more on similarity than wisdom.

If our instinct is to stay in the room when we smell smoke, we look for evidence that other people are electing to stay—not of people who may be urgently fleeing. And even when there is true expertise in our midst, as was the case in our earthquake experiments, we have a hard time seeing it if the expert is prescribing behavior that differs from that which we were prepared to do anyway. As a result, the normal effect of herding is amplification more than attenuation: People linger too long in the face of fire dangers, fuel rumors about pandemics, and collectively choose not to invest in building safer homes even when doing so has long-term benefits.

PART II

What We Can Do
to Improve Preparedness

Chapter 8

Overcoming the Biases
The Behavioral Risk Audit

Having made it this far in the book, you might rightfully surmise that we are not all that optimistic about the ability of people to make good protective decisions when faced with low-probability, high-consequence events. As decision makers, we look too little to the future when thinking about our choices, are too quick to forget the past, and try to overcome these limitations by imitating the behavior of other people who are just as prone to these flaws as we are. In addition, our tendency to be overly optimistic and impulsive, and to choose the status quo when we are unsure about what action to take, creates what could be called a perfect storm of potential decision errors. Our brains, we suggest, are simply not designed to think effectively about how to prepare for rare events that are beyond our domain of experience.

What makes matters worse is that if one looks at the landscape of modern approaches to preparedness, one sees little evidence that attempts are made to acknowledge, much less accommodate, these cognitive limitations. People residing in hazard-prone areas are provided with multipage checklists of preparedness measures they should consider, when in fact they are likely to adopt only one or two. People are urged to invest large amounts in building safer homes, when in fact they are likely to be discouraged by the time, cost, and resources required to get the project started; their mental time horizons for payback rarely extend beyond a year or two. Emergency management offices conduct training exercises designed to simulate disaster response, but these exercises tend to replicate how people will act when they have all their System 2 (deliberative) resources at their mental disposal—not the System 1 (instinctive) processes that will likely rule when a disaster is real. It is thus not surprising that well-intentioned preparedness plans often fail when put to the acid test.

A Possible Solution: The Behavioral Risk Audit

All is not lost, however. While we may not be able to alter how we think, knowledge of the decision biases discussed in this book might nevertheless be leveraged to anticipate how people and organizations may err when deciding how best to prepare for low-probability, high-consequence events. We can then formulate steps to mitigate these errors. We term this approach the *behavioral risk audit*. Like a financial audit, the behavioral risk audit is designed to provide communities and individuals with a systematic framework for characterizing their state of preparedness for different potential disasters, identify weak links, and suggest remedial solutions.

For novel disasters and hazards for which no existing preparedness plans exist (e.g., new pandemics or cyberterrorism), the audit is a tool for anticipating the biases that can arise when people think about the personal risks these disasters and hazards pose to them, their community, and other stakeholders. These biases, in turn, can then become the focal point of planning when preparedness tactics are designed. For well-known disasters and hazards (e.g., flood and storm risk), the audit provides a tool for identifying the tactical weak points of existing preparedness programs when they are put into practice.

The audit departs from existing practice in that it focuses on those who will be preparing for or responding to the hazard rather than on the hazard itself. Standard approaches start by analyzing the objective nature of the risk faced by individuals or communities, the vulnerability of the buildings and infrastructure, and then consider protective measures that people might take to mitigate that specific risk. The behavioral audit, in contrast, proceeds in reverse order: It starts by encouraging planners to think first about how individuals in hazard prone areas are likely to perceive risks and why they might *not* adopt different preparedness measures. Given this constraint, planners can then design preparedness plans that work *with* rather than *against* peoples' natural decision biases. In this way, the behavioral risk audit draws heavily on the principles of *choice architecture*, a term coined by Thaler and Sunstein[93] that highlights how people can be "nudged" into undertaking behaviors that benefit them by creating decision environments where better (in our case, safer) choices are the ones that come most naturally.

The Structure of the Audit

A behavioral risk audit consists of four steps of analysis for a given hazard context.

- **Step 1: List the biases.** List the six core psychological biases that underlie why people often underprepare for hazards in most contexts: myopia, amnesia, optimism, inertia, simplification, and herding.
- **Step 2: Describe impacts on beliefs.** Assess how each of the biases can lead to underestimation of the risks posed by a specific hazard.
- **Step 3: Analyze manifestation in preparedness.** Appraise how the misbeliefs about risk identified in step 2 can degrade the efficacy of different specific preparedness measures.
- **Step 4: Design remedies.** Design a suite of incentives and persuasive tactics to overcome the preparedness errors identified in step 3.

The outcome of the behavioral risk audit will be a problem-solution matrix that provides planners with an explanation of: the biases that can lead to distorted perceptions of risk, how misperceptions may be manifested in preparedness errors, and possible remedies. The general form of the problem-solution matrix is given in Table 8.1.

8.1. The Behavioral Risk Audit Problem-Solution Matrix

Bias	Impact on Beliefs	Manifestation in Preparedness	Remedy
Myopia: a tendency to plan over short future horizons	How might short-term thinking affect beliefs about the time available to prepare for a specific hazard?	If people focus on only the immediate future time horizon, which preparatory actions will be most threatened?	Tactics and incentives that lower the short-term costs of preparation
Amnesia: a tendency to base decisions on most recent experiences	What recent occurrence or nonoccurrence of the hazard might distort beliefs about the magnitude of the current threat?	Which specific protective investments are most likely to be overlooked if beliefs about risk rely too much on recent experience?	Communication tactics that correct distorted memories of the past
Optimism: a tendency to underestimate the likelihood of personal harm	Which risks posed by a hazard are the most likely to be under-estimated?	How would excessive optimism about specific risks inhibit specific protective measures?	Communication tactics that enhance beliefs about hazard likelihoods and impacts
Inertia: a tendency to choose default courses of action	What options form the "status quo" in preparation for the hazard?	If people are lured to choose default actions, which protective measures would be underinvested in?	Policies that make safer actions the default in a given setting
Simplification: a tendency to process only limited subsets of information	If individuals look to simplify their decision environment, which features of the hazard and preparation options will receive the greatest attention?	Are there essential preparatory measures that people might overlook?	Policies that simplify the set of preparedness choices faced by individuals
Herding: a tendency to make decisions by social imitation	What are social norms for preparedness in a given area for a given context?	How might a tendency to follow the herd distort collective decisions to invest in protection?	Tactics designed to foster stronger social norms of safety

In chapter 9, we will give a detailed example of how the audit might be applied in a given context. Note that the analysis is structured as a series of guided questions that would be considered by a planning team. For example, consider the bias of simplification (chapter 6), which is the inherent tendency for people to process only a small subset of the information available about a risk when making preparedness decisions. Here planners would be encouraged first to think about what a simplified view of a hazard might be from a homeowner's perspective. A homeowner faced with a hurricane threat might focus only on the wind threat posed by the storm. Given this, he would then be encouraged to think about what this would imply about the kind of preparedness mistakes he might make—such as forgetting to prepare for rain and flood risks. Finally, the discussion would shift to how to overcome such oversights without complicating the decision environment—for example, by recommending single essential actions that vary by location.

Implicit in the behavioral risk audit is the assumption that the biases in the at-risk population will vary by context. Everyone has his own Achilles' heel when it comes to making decisions about protection. For some people, it is myopia: They live in the moment and struggle to see wisdom in making protective investments whose payback lies in the future, no matter how compelling the appeal or how economically sensible it might seem to others. For others, it is unbridled optimism: No matter how urgent the warnings are, they see risks from hazards as something that will happen to others, not themselves. As such, the output of a behavioral risk audit will not be the recommendation of a single remedy for enhancing preparedness, but rather a *suite* of measures designed to target the different biases of a population of individuals, each with his own psychic flaws.

Finally, it is important to emphasize that the audit is not envisioned as a one-time exercise, but rather one that is continually revisited and revised as protection plans are developed. In the early stages of planning, for example, the audit provides a tool for envisioning hazards and existing preparedness measures through the eyes of stakeholders, while in later stages, it would be used to assess the sufficiency of existing policies.

Chapter 9

The Behavioral Risk Audit in Action
The Case of Flood Risk

To illustrate how a behavioral risk audit would proceed, we consider how it can be used to develop a comprehensive approach to encouraging more widespread adoption of insurance against flood risks.

Setting the Scene: Flood Risk

Flood insurance has a checkered history in the United States. In 1897 a newly established company in Cairo, Illinois, made the first attempt to provide insurance coverage. The firm had no trouble attracting customers; there had been enormous property damage during the previous two years, from floods on the Missouri and Mississippi Rivers. During 1898 the company was highly profitable, but severe flooding the following year produced claims that exceeded the premiums and the firm's capital, and even washed the home office away. During the late 1920s, 30 companies decided to offer flood insurance again, but the Mississippi floods of 1927 and additional flooding the following year caused such large losses that no private insurer wanted to offer coverage for the next 40 years, which led to the passage of the National Flood Insurance Program (NFIP).

Congress passed the NFIP in 1968 to provide government-backed insurance protection to Americans living in flood-prone areas. The impetus for this legislation was the escalating costs of post-disaster relief triggered initially by the Alaska earthquake of 1964, and followed by severe flooding and damage from Hurricane Betsy in 1965, America's first billion-dollar hurricane. The NFIP offered highly subsidized premiums to homeowners currently residing in flood-prone communities willing to institute building codes and land-use regulation. Residents moving into these areas were required to pay risk-based rates to discourage them from locating to high-hazard areas.

Homeowners were expected to purchase insurance voluntarily, but few actually took advantage of the subsidies, which sometimes were as high as 90 percent of the risk-based rate. For this reason, Congress required property owners to purchase flood insurance if they had a federally insured mortgage and were in a flood-prone community that had joined the NFIP. One would think that this legislation passed in 1972 would have created a large demand for insurance, but that was not the case. The reality is that, today, most homeowners in flood-prone areas are uninsured against water-related damage.

Developing a Problem-Solution Matrix for Flood Risk

We will now illustrate how we might develop a problem-solution matrix for the case of flood risk, by considering each of the six biases in turn, and discussing their impact, manifestation in preparedness, and possible remedies.

1. Overcoming the Myopia Bias

In chapter 2 we explain how there is a tendency for individuals to focus on short time horizons when making decisions with respect to preparing for future disasters. The impact of this bias on decisions about protecting against flood risk is straightforward: Because floods are rare events, most homeowners will think of them as a threat that lies only in the distant future, not one that needs to be attended to immediately. Because flood-protection measures that would reduce the need for insurance have high up-front costs (e.g., flood proofing, elevating a home), a homeowner whose mental time horizon stretches over only two to three years will thus have a hard time justifying such expenditures, and will underinvest in mitigation.

Given that myopia is a hard-wired bias, the most promising remedies would be those that reveal its existence, and address it by reducing the pain of paying for mitigation up front. For example, one solution might be long-term loans tied to a mortgage that spread the cost of this risk reduction measure over time. As an example, in 2014, the state of Connecticut stepped up to the plate by initiating its Shore Up CT program. Residential or business property owners are able to obtain 15-year loans ranging from $10,000 to $300,000 at an annual interest rate of 2¾% to elevate structures, retrofit properties with additional flood protection, or assist with wind-proofing structures on property prone to coastal flooding.

Long-term loans to homes and businesses for mitigation can also help aid myopia by lowering the cost of insurance—and thus give people a sense that they are receiving immediate benefits. Consider a homeowner who is faced with a $25,000 cost to retrofit his house so it is less prone to flood damage. If flood insurance were risk-based, the annual premium would decrease from $4,000 to $520, a $3,480 reduction in costs. A 15-year loan for $25,000 at an annual interest rate of 2¾% would result in loan payments of $2,040 per year, so the savings to the homeowner each year would be $1,440 (i.e., $3,480 - $2,040).

2. Overcoming the Amnesia Bias

In chapter 3 we discuss how people are, by nature, trial-and-error learners with short memories, and how this can cause "disaster cycles," where we invest in protection shortly after a disaster but then withdraw those investments as the years pass without another disaster. Disasters are rare and protection is costly. Over time our brains teach us the wrong lesson, as expenditures on insurance policies and the like are increasingly seen as unpleasant acts that convey no reward. In the context of flood risk, this bias has a simple impact and manifestation: an increasing tendency for the perceived benefits of insurance to decline over time, eventually leading to its cancellation—a decision that will, of course, be regretted when the next flood eventually arrives.

Since people can't be trained to have better memories, the best solution here would be, in essence, to flip the reward structure so that the recent *absence* of a claim is seen as a positive event that encourages rather than discourages renewal—that is, convince people that *the best return on their policy is no return at all*. One tangible means of doing this might be to give people a $100 reward at the end of a claim-free year in the form of a restaurant chit so they can celebrate having had no return on their policy. By giving them a rebate and reminding them that they have a reason to feel good, residents in hazard-prone areas are likely to renew their insurance policy for another year. At the very least, insurance renewal bills should come packaged with vivid literature that reminds people *why* they are buying this insurance, for example, because of the flood-proneness of the area they live in.

Another complementary remedy would be to design communication plans aimed at keeping memories of past disasters alive—in essence, bringing the past closer to the present. As we illustrate in chapter 3, however, this can be difficult when disasters are truly rare and when decision makers have no personal memories that can be queued. The tsunami warning monuments near Miyako did little to dissuade rebuilding in coastal Japan after previous disasters, and the Galveston Sea Wall, a standing monument to the great 1900 hurricane, has done little to dissuade unprotected development on barrier islands. In contrast, when there have been more recent disasters, communication campaigns that carry vivid images of what those disasters were like can at least help extend memories to support longer-duration investments in protection, such as infrastructure projects.

3. Overcoming the Optimism Bias

In chapter 4 we note that there is a natural human tendency to view one's current situation in the best possible light. Even a homeowner who is aware she lives in a flood zone tends to believe she will be spared, or that if there is a flood, the consequences will not be severe. This sense of optimism is often fueled by our inability to have a good mental grasp on the meaning of very small probabilities. While, for example, we might have a good sense of the risk that comes with a coin toss, this is unlikely to be the case if we are told that the risk of our homes being affected by a flood is 1 in 100 years. Given this ambiguity, our natural tendency to be optimists—"disasters can't happen to me"—causes us to underappreciate true risk. Again, the impact and manifestation on flood protection is clear: a tendency to underestimate the personal risk and thus underinvest in protective measures.

One approach that can help people gain a better understanding of low probabilities is to present those probabilities using a longer time frame. People are more willing to wear seat belts if they are told they have a one-in-three chance of being in an automobile accident over a 50-year lifetime of driving, rather than a 1-in-100,000 chance on each trip they take.[94] Similarly, if a homeowner is considering flood protection over the 25-year life of a home, she is far more likely to take the risk seriously if told that the chance of at least one severe flood occurring during this time period is greater than 1 in 5, rather than 1 in 100 in any given year.[95] Framing the probability using a longer time horizon should be attractive to insurers and real estate agents who want to encourage their clients to invest in protective measures.

Likewise, people may be better able to evaluate low-probability risks if they are described in terms of a familiar concrete context. For example, individuals might not understand what a 1-in-500 probability means, but may have a better understanding if it is described as being a bit lower than the odds that a woman will give birth to twins (1 in 70). To illustrate this effect, one of the authors conducted an experiment in which respondents were given three scenarios: a chemical plant for which the likelihood of a person dying from the discharge of a toxic vapor cloud was 1 in 650, a chemical plant for which that likelihood was 1 in 6,300, and a plant for which it was 1 in 68,000. When the probabilities were described in those abstract terms, respondents were *unable* to differentiate among the facilities in terms of their riskiness. However, when these same probabilities were described along with a concrete example comparing the likelihood of a person dying in a car accident on a windy snowy road in Colorado (1 in 5,900) with the chances of dying in an accident on a straight road in Arizona (1 in 66,000), they could now easily differentiate the relative riskiness of the chemical plants.[96]

4. Overcoming the Inertia Bias

When a person is unsure about the best course of action, there is a tendency to look for a default option, a simple heuristic for escaping the difficult task of appraising the pros and cons of the alternatives. This problem is particularly acute for flood risk: the probability that a flood will occur in a specific location in a given year is ambiguous, the damage that would occur highly uncertain, and planning horizons rarely known for sure. When faced with such uncertainty there is a tendency to avoid the decision altogether, choosing to accept the status quo of no protection.

As pointed out in chapter 5, field and controlled experiments in behavioral economics reveal that consumers are more likely to stick with the default option rather than going to the trouble of opting out in favor of some other alternative. To date, this framing technique has been applied to situations where the outcome is either known with certainty or when the chosen option, such as a recommended 401(k) plan, has a higher expected return than the other options.[97]

Applying this to the context of flood insurance would require a mechanism by which people living in flood-prone areas can decline flood insurance, but only by explicitly *opting out* of the default option of having coverage. One way in which this could be implemented would be for flood insurance to be bundled with the standard set of services paid for with real estate taxes, such as sewer systems and roads. A resident who does not want the coverage, however, could apply for a rebate. Such a policy, of course, would likely encounter political headwinds, but based on prior research, it would likely significantly increase the percentage of homeowners holding flood insurance policies.

Building codes, of course, are the most well-known example of use of defaults, and we explore their advantages (and downsides) in more detail in the next chapter. In essence, building codes make safer homes the status quo in a community. Most state building codes, for example, now require owners of homes built in special flood zones both to elevate their property's lowest level and to allow water to flow freely below that (e.g., by constructing the home on stilts).[98] The challenge, of course, is that they only work if the *quality* and strength of codes are constantly being revisited and revised by policy makers, ideally *before* disasters occur, not after. And therein lies a danger: Building codes are often slow to be revised because they themselves are prone to status-quo biases; when policy makers are unsure how and when to modify codes, there is the tendency to leave the current ones intact.

5. Overcoming the Simplification Bias

As we discussed in chapter 6, when people are faced with the complexities that typically accompany protective decisions there is an innate tendency to look for ways to simplify—basing decisions on only a small subset of factors that fully contribute to safety. If left to their own devices this editing process can lead to poor choices. The work-around is thus to create simpler decision environments, removing the need to make complex decisions in the first place.

As an example, one of the authors recently proposed that insurers consider offering homeowners multiyear flood insurance policies, thus freeing them from the need to make an annual decision about renewal. Flood policies would be written for three-to five-year terms that would be tied to the structure rather than the property owner, and would carry an annual premium reflecting risk that would remain stable for the length of the contract. Property owners who cancelled their insurance early would incur a penalty cost in the same way that those who refinance their houses have to pay a cancellation cost to the bank issuing the mortgage. The big advantage would be simplicity—rather than the homeowner having to deliberate each year about whether he should renew or worrying if he is insured should a flood occur, coverage would be automatic.

Of course, the pragmatic feasibility of such a program would depend on whether consumer demand for the product would be sufficient to convince FEMA to devote time and money into developing and marketing it. To investigate this, an online experiment was conducted with adults over 30 in which they were asked to choose between one-year and two-year contracts to insure themselves against losses from hurricane-related damage. The two-year contract had a stable premium over time, while the one-year contact had a lower premium in year one but a premium that could be higher in year two if the homeowner suffered damage from a hurricane in the first year. A large majority of the respondents preferred the two-year contract over the one-year contract because it guaranteed the same premium over time, even when the total premium for the two-year contract was priced higher than the actuarially fair price for two one-year policies. Introducing a two-year insurance contract also increased the aggregate demand for disaster insurance.[99]

6. Overcoming the Herd Bias

In the end, the most cost-effective means of elevating safety may be through social norms. If residents in flood-prone areas learn that all their neighbors are making investments in flood proofing and insurance, they are likely to follow suit. But is it possible to create such norms when none currently exist? One novel approach currently being employed by the Insurance Institute for Business and Home Safety is to award seals of approval to homes that meet or exceed building code standards. The hope is that such a seal of approval could not only increase the property value of a home, but also be seen as a sign of status by others in the community—nudging them to undertake improvements.

Evidence from a July 1994 telephone survey of 1,241 residents in six hurricane-prone areas on the Atlantic and Gulf coasts provides supporting evidence that there might be widespread support for some type of seal of approval. More than 90% of respondents felt that local home builders should be required to adhere to building codes, and 85% considered it very important that local building departments conduct inspections of new residential construction.[100]

The Summary Schematic

The final step in the behavioral risk audit is to develop a schematic that provides an integrative view of the analyses done in steps one through four mentioned in the previous chapter: the listing of biases, their impact, their manifestation, and remedies. An example for the case of flood insurance is shown in the problem-solution matrix in Table 9.1.

In addition to summarizing the behavioral impediments to adopting protective measures, a problem-solution matrix such as the

Table 9.1. Behavioral Risk Audit Problem-Solution Matrix for Reducing Future Flood Losses

Bias	Impact on Beliefs	Manifestation in Preparedness	Remedy
Myopia: a tendency to plan over short future horizons	Focus on short-term horizons in evaluating flood loss mitigation options	Failure to invest in cost-effective measures due to high upfront costs	Couple long-term loans with insurance premium reductions to spread the upfront cost over time.
Amnesia: a tendency to base decisions on most recent experiences	Fading memory of past floods and resulting damage	Failure to renew annual flood insurance policy	Automatically renew multi-year policies with constant annual premiums.
Optimism: a tendency to underestimate the likelihood of personal harm	Underestimation of the probability of a flood	Tendency to see flood insurance and mitigation as overly expensive relative to benefits	Stretch time horizon so individual perceives the probability of a disaster to be closer to the scientific estimate.
Inertia: a tendency to choose default courses of action	A preference for the status quo in protective investments; for floods, doing nothing	Reluctance to purchase insurance or invest in existing loss-reduction measures (e.g., purchased storm shutters); procrastination in decision making	Make protection the default; make insurance a condition for obtaining a mortgage, or part of a bundled policy the resident can opt out of.
Simplification: a tendency to process only limited subsets of information	Limited consideration of information available about flood risk	Ignorance of the flood risk at a location; lack of knowledge of possible remedies	Implement communication programs that make it easier for residents to be aware of their flood risk, providing examples of the consequences of floods that dramatize impact.
Herding: a tendency to make decisions by social imitation	Tendency to base insurance decision on whether friends and neighbors have flood policies	Low rates of take-up at the community level	Implement communication programs that emphasize social norms of safety; offer seals of approval that enhance the social status of protective investments.

one in Table 9.1 encourages planners to consider the *interactions* that naturally exist among different measures. As an example, myopia might be addressed by offering residents multiyear insurance policies with automatic renewal—policies communicating risk messages that highlight the likelihood of a future flood by stretching the time horizon and constructing worst-case scenarios should one not invest in protective measures.

Recap: Use and Limitations of the Behavioral Audit

In this chapter, we illustrate how the behavioral risk audit can be used to reduce future flood losses. Consider a community whose approach to managing flood risk is, first, to provide enriched information about the steps that could be taken to reduce flood damage and, second, to offer property tax rebates for homeowners who undertake those measures. In this case, the audit might proceed in the *reverse* order of that which we have discussed: Working with a schematic template such as that in Table 9.1, planners would start by asking themselves what biases these programs would help overcome and, more critically, what biases the programs do *not* address.

In this chapter, we've provided an example of how the behavioral risk audit could be used to develop a comprehensive strategy for overcoming biases associated with relatively short-term risk, floods. But how might it be applied to help planning for truly long-run risks, such as climate change, where the hazards are those to be faced by decision makers who have yet to be born? In the concluding chapter, we take up this question.

Chapter 10

Protection in the Truly Long Run

When the residents of the Bolivar Peninsula in Texas returned home after Hurricane Ike in 2008 they were met by a landscape that bore little resemblance to the one they had left just a few days earlier. What was once a community of rustic vacation homes was now a wasteland of cement slabs, pilings, and crumpled asphalt. Survivors picked through the rubble to try to recover what they could, but for most of them, it was a lost cause: Almost everything that was not bolted down had been washed into Galveston Bay. It was hard to imagine that life could ever return to what it was before.

Yet it did, and far more quickly than most would have imagined. Within two years the debris had been cleared away, and new construction was already beginning to appear. By 2015, real estate developers were bragging about how the Bolivar Peninsula was back, and in a big way.[101] What were once small cabins had given way to new $750,000 luxury beach homes. To further reinforce the idea that Ike was a thing of the past, millions of cubic yards of sand had been piped in to restore the beach. Visitors to the area today would have a hard time imagining the destruction that occurred there just eight years ago.

The story of the rebuilding of the Bolivar Peninsula is, of course, a heartening one that demonstrates the remarkable resilience of people to disasters, something that is often seen after similar events worldwide. But we suggest that these outward signs of recovery are something of an illusion. While houses were indeed rebuilt, little has been done to lower the fundamental risk that caused the destruction. Homes there today are just as much at risk from destruction by the sea as before, with perhaps even more value being placed in harm's way. It is just a matter of time before another Ike hits the area, inducing another cycle of destruction, another cycle of government recovery aid, another cycle of rebuilding.

Up to this point in the book we have focused on explaining why individuals often make poor decisions about protection, and have outlined the steps that can be taken to overcome these errors. Yet, by studying decisions solely at the level of the individual, we overlook a major piece of the protection puzzle: the fact that the responsibility for safety lies in the hands not just of individuals, but also elected officials concerned with disasters' impacts on the general public. To achieve greater safety in places such as the Bolivar Peninsula, decisions need to be made at scales that extend beyond the time horizons and control of individuals: legislation restricting development on barrier islands, improved building codes, and investment of public funds in the construction of protective infrastructure (such as seawalls). These collective decisions reflect society's willingness to think about risk in both the short and long run, make the investments needed to manage it, and understand the public welfare implications of these decisions.

In this concluding chapter, we discuss preparing for risks at a societal level, with a focus on the long-run benefits and costs of these actions. Using a hazard on the horizon that has proven particularly challenging, sea level rise, we'll explore how to encourage communities to embrace cultures of protective action.

Setting the Scene: Rising Seas

Among the many possible negative consequences of climate change, sea level rise is the least controversial. Since reliable records began in the 1800s, sea levels have been steadily rising worldwide, something that poses an obvious risk to the trillions of dollars in real estate that now sit at our coastlines. Yet, sea level rise is also a deceptively subtle hazard. While sea levels are indeed steadily rising, that rise is at such a slow rate, about three millimeters a year, that it would likely go unnoticed by all but the sharpest of eyes. The Miami and New York City waterfronts today, for example, look pretty much the same as they did a century ago. Ships still land at the same ports, waterfront parks are as reliably dry today as they were in the past.

Yet there are strong indications that this is about to change. The consensus among climate scientists is that we are soon approaching an irreversible "tipping point" in the rate of sea level rise, such that by the turn of the next century, sea levels may be three feet (or more) higher than they are today.[102] Such an increase would not just require the relocation of vast numbers of people and infrastructure currently adjacent to the coast, but also create a wide range of spillover effects, including amplification of the effects of storm surges and, in the case of South Florida, seawater intrusion into the local fresh groundwater supply.

While this threat is a very real one, the good news is that we have plenty of time, at least in principle, to prepare for it. In South Florida, for example, there is ample time for builders and city planners to start the slow process of elevating streets and buildings, installing pumping technologies, and planning for the construction of desalination plants to deal with saltwater intrusion in the water supply. Better yet, because in Florida the money for such preventive actions needs to come from real estate tax revenue, the fact that the threat is some years off should allow the area to sustain its appeal to tourists and investors, filling the coffers with the money needed to pay for it all. Unlike the highly uncertain hazards that most of our book has focused on, one might think sea level rise would be an easy risk to manage: We know it's coming, and we have the time and resources to deal with it preemptively.

But if you have been paying attention to the lessons of this book, what we are about to say won't surprise you: None of this is happening. Planners in coastal cities are sounding the alarms, but the pleas to take action are widely falling on deaf ears. The City of Miami Beach, for example, recently invested $400 million to build pumps to deal with the increase in nuisance flooding that has been seen in recent years, but the investment is designated only to remedy the problem as it exists today, not the much larger problems that will come as the century wears on.[103] The City of New York has approved spending to prepare for sea level rise, but all in anticipation of a two-foot rise by the end of the century, not the three-foot rise that most climate scientists warn about.[104]

Why the apparent lack of concern? To some degree this is another example of the harmful effects of the six biases we have been exploring in this book, but now applied at a societal level. It is hard for politicians to see wisdom in large capital outlays for benefits that will be realized long after they have left office (myopia); the uncertainty that exists in the exact magnitude of sea level rise breeds a bias toward the status quo of doing nothing (inertia); and the fact that most cities are taking a similar wait-and-see approach is misconstrued as evidence that the officials in those other cities know what they are doing (a destructive herd effect).

Yet there is something more at work here, a factor that makes overcoming these biases in this case potentially even more intractable. Community-level adaptations to the future effects of sea level rise will require substantial inflows of new capital, and that can happen only if individuals see short-term personal benefits emerging from such investments—enough to support increases in property taxes, enough to undertake costly adaptations on their own. Yet a resident who sits down with pen and paper and tries to calculate the economic return on such investment—the kind of deliberative System 2 thinking that we would normally advocate—will likely find that the numbers just don't add up. The effects of sea level rise are just too far off, the parameters too unknowable. Persuasion in this case would seem to require appeals to morality more than money, conscience more than calculation. Needless to say, this can be a hard ask.

Taking Preventive Action: Four Guiding Principles

This conundrum, of course, is by no means limited to sea level rise. Climate change poses a broad range of other threats whose consequences lie beyond the planning horizons of current residents, and our society faces long-term social and economic risks that are similarly difficult to fathom. Yet ignoring these risks is clearly an unacceptable option. We have a moral responsibility to care for future generations, even in the absence of immediate paybacks to ourselves.

How might we achieve this? We argue for collective agreement on a set of higher-level *guiding principles* for risk management that are accepted both by policy makers and the affected public.

To illustrate, a resident might normally be hard-pressed to favor a tax hike to pay for improvements in infrastructure in her community if the threat is perceived to be decades into the future. She is more likely to see the merits of these improvements if they are tied to achieving the long-term preservation of the human species, a goal to which she subscribes.

We propose four guiding principles as an umbrella for how societies should approach the management of long-term risk:

Guiding principle 1: Commit to long-term protective planning as a major priority. This principle, of course, is fundamental; decision makers in the public and private sector need to place reduction in future losses and the required investments in protection near the top of their agendas, and provide rationales for individuals to support their proposals.

Guiding principle 2: Commit to policies that discourage individual and community actions that increase their exposure to

long-term risks. The simplest means of managing risk is to avoid it. Policies regulating land use, building codes, and insurance need to be designed to reflect the expected benefits and costs associated with exposure to future risks. Insurers should be permitted to price their coverage to reflect the nature of the risk and encourage those at risk to invest in loss-reduction measures. Building codes could complement insurance by requiring structures to meet specific standards.

Guiding principle 3: Create policies that consider the cognitive biases that inhibit adoption of protective measures. Regulatory policies designed to dissuade risk exposure will be effective only if they are widely adopted and enforced. The key lesson of this book is that people are naturally prone to a range of biases that inhibit long-term thinking. Therefore, policies have to be designed in ways that recognize and overcome these biases.

Guiding principle 4: Commit to addressing problems equitably. A transformative shift toward long-term protection will lead to costs that will differentially impact different groups in society. Long-term protective policies must be designed with these inequalities in mind, addressing the hardships faced by low- and middle-income households facing budget constraints, so that those households have economic incentives to adopt the protective measures.

Strategies for the Case of Sea Level Rise

To illustrate how these guiding principles might be used to develop strategies for dealing with truly long-term risks such as sea level rise, let's return to the problems faced by the Bolivar Peninsula and other coastal communities in Texas. As we have seen, this is an area that has long been prone to periodic hurricane hazards, but rising seas will make the problem measurably worse over the coming decades. Whereas in the past it took a severe hurricane such as Ike to impose major flood damage, in the coming decades even the smallest of storms could induce severe flooding, increasing the likelihood from an every-50-years problem to one that occurs every five years.

How should Texas deal with this increase in the odds of severe flooding? Any set of policies that relies on people adapting to sea level rise on their own will likely prove ineffective. Even when risks are well known and relatively close at hand, such as the risk of hurricanes as it exists today, people have a hard time seeing beyond the next year or two (myopia), and underestimate the likelihood that they themselves will suffer harm. Yet here we are dealing with a much more ambiguous risk, one that is perhaps 30 years or more off—beyond the time horizons of home mortgages and even beyond some lifetimes. As such, many of the nudges that we suggest in the previous chapter for encouraging people to better prepare for the flood risk they currently face (such as better communication) are unlikely to be sufficient for dealing with a hazard that is truly distant. For example, it could be that if we fully educate Texas residents about the current best estimates on the timing and scale of sea level rise, it might simply reinforce their intuition that it is a distant threat best left for the next generation of homeowners to deal with.

A closer review of the problem would suggest another path: design policies that create *decision environments* that foster protection (guiding principle 2), but where individuals do not need to make personal decisions about the value of protection.

Designing Policies for Better Decision Making

We are naturally led to protective decisions by the latter three of our six major biases: inertia, simplification, and herding. Such decision environments might be marked by four major features.

1. Well-enforced regulations and standards

The idea that people have difficulty seeing the benefits of voluntary investment in long-term residential safety is hardly a new one, and this forms the basis of the most widely adopted protective measures: well-enforced regulations and standards by either the private or public sector that ensure safety, with any violations subject to penalties or fines. In the case of natural disasters, for example, banks and financial institutions require homeowners' insurance that covers wind damage from tornados and hurricanes as a condition for borrowers' obtaining a mortgage. Likewise, as pointed out in chapter 8, the federal government requires insurance to cover flood damage through the National Flood Insurance Program (NFIP) if the property in the affected floodplain has a federally insured mortgage.

But such regulations are hardly universal. In the case of earthquakes, the private sector determined that it could not continue to offer coverage against this risk after suffering severe losses from the Northridge earthquake in 2004. The California Earthquake Authority now offers insurance. But banks do not require this coverage as a condition for obtaining a mortgage.

Building codes are another common way to make safety a default, but they come with a downside: They are of little help if they are not rigorously enforced. Prior to Hurricane Andrew in Florida in 1992, for example, the state had a strong building code in place, but tremendous damage still occurred due to the lack of enforcement, particularly in newer homes in the area. Likewise, building codes typically require property owners to meet standards on new structures, but normally do not require them to retrofit existing structures. Often such codes are necessary, particularly when property owners are not inclined to adopt mitigation measures on their own due to their misperception of the expected benefits and/or their inclination to underestimate the probability of a disaster occurring.

To address such problems, building codes need to be accompanied by policies that oversee their scope and rigor. One current example is the Building Code Effectiveness Grading Schedule (BCEGS), a community-level mitigation rating system administered by the Insurance Services Office (ISO). The BCEGS assesses the building codes in effect in a particular community and how the community enforces building codes, putting special emphasis on mitigation of losses from floods, hurricanes, tornadoes, and earthquakes. The BCEGS score is based not only on the building code in place, but also on field inspector staffing and qualifications.

The BCEGS ratings received by communities are provided to insurers to use as an underwriting tool. Few insurance companies are using the BCEGS report to provide premium discounts. The one notable exception is Florida, where insurers are required by law to offer discounts on wind protection premiums based on a community's BCEGS rating. Communities that do not participate in the program are assessed a 1% surcharge on wind protection premiums.[105]

2. Zoning Ordinances

One of the more vexing problems facing policy makers after major catastrophes is whether to permit reconstruction in areas that have been damaged. Knowing that sea level rise will only make flood events more common, it would seem prudent to limit rebuilding. Unfortunately, this is easier said and proposed than done. Both after Hurricane Ike in the Bolivar Peninsula and after Hurricane Katrina in New Orleans and other areas, there was strong political support for rebuilding homes in the same places where they were damaged or destroyed. Indeed, not to do so somehow seems to show a lack of empathy for those who have lived part of if not all their lives in the area. As the argument goes, they have family and social connections there; for many of them, nowhere else could be home.[106]

What exacerbates this problem is that when rebuilding occurs, there is a tendency for it to happen in a way that removes all signs that might communicate to new and prospective residents the inherent risks posed by the location. As with the rebuilding that occurred after Hurricane Ike, visitors to the Mississippi Gulf Coast today will find little evidence of the complete devastation the area suffered from Hurricane Katrina in 2005. Attractive mansions are once again strung along Route 90, and sandy beaches offer little clue as to this being perhaps the most hazard-prone section of coastline in the United States.[107]

3. Buyouts for Relocating Homes

One tool for combating this tendency to rebuild in areas prone to recurrent losses is buy-back programs that award owners with cash for destroyed properties on the condition that the lots not be rebuilt. After Hurricane Ike devastated Texas, for example, FEMA spent $103 million on such a program, buying back 756 destroyed homes and converting the remaining land to parkland.[108]

The challenge of such programs, of course, is securing compliance from homeowners. In cases where the properties are second homes, vacation residences, this might be easy, but when the homes are primary residences, it can be challenging, as individuals may be loath to move away from a community of neighbors with whom they've lived for years. To illustrate, a 2013 survey conducted among residents in New York and New Jersey who had just experienced the devastation of Hurricane Sandy indicated that most believed that federal aid was best spent on rebuilding homes rather than buying them.[109] Given such resistance, decisions to accept buyouts requires community-level support, where residents agree to relocate as a group rather than as individuals.

A good example of such an effort occurred in Staten Island after Hurricane Sandy in 2012. Two weeks after the storm, Joseph Tirone, who owned a rental property in Oakwood Beach, decided to get everyone to agree to leave their damaged homes and relocate elsewhere. Almost all the residents who attended the meeting he organized indicated that they would be interested in selling and leaving if they could get a fair price for their houses and be assured that their homes would not be given to rich people or be redeveloped into new homes.

In January 2013, only four months after Sandy, New York State governor Andrew Cuomo praised the community for coming together, and committed to using home relocation funds from FEMA's Hazard Mitigation Grant Program (HMGP), which mandates that the land be returned to open space—the same program that had funded land-reclamation projects after Hurricane Ike five years earlier.[110] Similar programs were authorized by New Jersey governor Chris Christie on an even larger scale: The state's "Blue Acres" buyout program allocated $300 million to acquire 719 severely damaged properties across several municipalities, and by 2015, more than 500 offers had been accepted by homeowners, all carrying the agreement that the lots not be rebuilt.[111]

It is difficult enough to convince residents in a community to relocate to safer areas after a disaster unless there is a funded program such as those put in place by FEMA after Ike and Sandy. An even more difficult challenge is convincing them to move *prior* to a disaster, when there are no funds available and few incentives for them to do so, either at a social level (leaving friends and neighbors) or an economic one (selling their property at a price that enables them to buy a new home).

4. Long-term tax incentives

A final example of how communities might encourage forward-looking building practices is through the provision of long-term tax incentives. Much in the same way that cities often use tax abatements to encourage development of blighted areas, abatements (and possibly surcharges) can be used to steer development away from high-risk barrier islands to safer areas farther inland. Tax incentives might also be used to persuade individuals to invest in adaptation on their own. For example, if a homeowning taxpayer installs a mitigation measure that would reduce the likelihood of losses from a flood or other disaster, he would get a rebate on state taxes to reflect the lower cost of disaster relief, or his property taxes could be reduced.

While tax incentives might help spur adaptation, care needs to be taken to ensure that they don't generate externalities that discourage it. As an example, a property owner who improves a home by making it safer may well have the property reassessed at a higher value and would thus be faced with a higher rather than a lower tax bill. California has recognized this problem, and in 1990 voters in that state passed Proposition 127, which exempts buildings that have undergone seismic rehabilitation improvements from reassessments that would increase property taxes.

Berkeley has taken an additional step to encourage homebuyers to retrofit newly purchased homes by instituting a transfer tax rebate. The city has a 1.5% tax levied on property transfer transactions; up to one-third of this amount can be applied to seismic upgrades during the sale of a property. Qualifying upgrades include foundation repairs or replacement, wall bracing in basements, shear wall installation, water heater anchoring, and securing of chimneys.[112]

The Dilemma of Affordability

While it might be possible to create safer environments through a cocktail of stronger building codes, risk-based insurance pricing, and zoning restrictions, this has to be done in a way that does not impose differential hardships on residents with more limited means—the last of our four guiding principles for taking preventative action. For example, if one demands that flood insurance be priced in a way that reflects the true risk of a location (guiding principle 2), then some low- and middle-income residents whose insurance is currently subsidized will be unable to obtain coverage against that risk. To illustrate the impact of risk-based insurance on homeowners' ability to pay, consider the owner of a single-family home in Tottenville, Staten Island, who currently has a subsidized annual insurance premium of $1,400. If the premium were risk-based, it would jump to $9,500, and that homeowner might be hard-pressed to pay for this coverage.[113] This example raises challenges for developing strategies for dealing with issues of inequality and affordability.

One way to maintain risk-based insurance premiums while at the same time addressing issues of affordability is to offer means-tested vouchers or tax credits that cover part of the cost of insurance.[114] Several existing programs could serve as models for developing such a voucher system: the Supplemental Nutrition Assistance Program (SNAP, also known as food stamps), the Low Income Home Energy Assistance Program (LIHEAP), and the Universal Service Fund (USF). The value of the voucher or tax credit would be based on current income and would be determined by a specific set of criteria as outlined in a recent study by the National Research Council.[115]

Of course, the dilemma posed by such subsidies, however humane, is that, by definition, they do little to achieve the long-term goal of reducing collective risk exposure. Indeed, some might see them as creating a different kind of inequity: Those with higher incomes, who do not get subsidies, receive clear signals about the risk of their locations, while those with lower incomes are implicitly encouraged to remain in harm's way. As such, need-based means-tested voucher programs and the like must be viewed as transitional repairs, eventually to be coupled with incentives to relocate to areas that face lower risk, particularly as disaster risks escalate in the coming decades.

Postscript
The Ostrich Paradox Revisited

There are many reasons that those in harm's way do not protect themselves against natural disasters. In this book, we have highlighted behavioral considerations that include short memories when thinking about the past, short horizons when planning for the future, and a tendency to make decisions by imitating the behavior of others who are no less prone to these biases than we are. All these effects limit people's interest in and ability to invest in protective measures—something that carries costs that are borne by not just individuals but also society as a whole.

If we as a society are to commit ourselves to reducing future losses from natural and man-made disasters in the truly long run, we need to do more than hope that individuals and policy makers will see wisdom in these investments on their own. Rather, we need to engage the private and public sectors in innovative partnerships that create environments where safety is the social norm, encouraged by appropriate regulations and well-enforced standards, and where the costs of this transformation are equitably distributed across society—ideas that follow from the four guiding principles proposed in chapter 10.

The challenge, however, is how to get from here to there. Although protective policies that address long-term problems such as climate change are widely embraced in principle, they still require remedies for overcoming the biases that cause people to look the other way when hazards loom. This can be a difficult task if, when faced with risk, people bury their heads in the sand like the infamous ostrich the title of this book references, or if they lack the cognitive wherewithal to properly adapt to that risk when it is acknowledged.

Our key argument is that there *is* a way out, but the path there carries a certain paradox: As individuals and planners, we need to be *more* like ostriches, not less. That is, in the same way that the ostrich has adapted its behavior to take into consideration its *physical* limitations, we humans, when thinking about risk, need to develop policies that take into consideration our inherent *cognitive* limitations.

Notes

1   Neil Frank, "The Great Galveston Hurricane," in *Hurricane: Coping with Disaster*, ed. Robert Simpson (Washington, DC: American Geophysical Union, 2003), 129–40.

2   Willie Drye, "Hurricane Ike's 9-foot Floods to Bring 'Certain Death,'" *National Geographic News*, September 12, 2008, http://news.nationalgeographic.com/news/2008/09/080912-hurricane-ike.html.

3   FEMA, "Hurricane Ike Impact Report," December 2008, https://www.fema.gov/pdf/hazard/hurricane/2008/ike/impact_report.pdf.

4   Wikipedia, "List of Natural Disasters by Death Toll: 52 Deadliest Earthquakes," https://en.wikipedia.org/wiki/List_of_natural_disasters_by_death_toll#52_deadliest_earthquakes.

5   "Tragic Donegal Man's Sons Are Washed from Mother's Arms During Hurricane Sandy," *Donegal Daily*, November 5, 2012, http://www.donegaldaily.com/2012/11/05/tragic-donegal-mans-sons-are-washed-from-mothers-arms-during-hurricane-sandy/.

6   Michael Sedon, "Staten Island Weeps at Discovery of 2 Little Bodies," silive.com, November 2, 2012 http://www.silive.com/news/index.ssf/2012/11/staten_island_weeps_at_discove.html.

7   National Hurricane Center advisory bulletin, "Hurricane Sandy," http://www.nhc.noaa.gov/archive/2012/al18/al182012.public.030.shtml.

8   James Barron, Joseph Goldstein, and Kirk Semple, "Staten Island Was Tragic Epicenter of Storm's Casualties," *New York Times*, November 1, 2012, http://www.nytimes.com/2012/11/02/nyregion/staten-island-was-tragic-epicenter-of-new-york-citys-storm-casualties.html?_r=1&.

9   "Mapping Hurricane Sandy's Deadly Toll," *New York Times*, November 17, 2012, http://www.nytimes.com/interactive/2012/11/17/nyregion/hurricane-sandy-map.html?_r=0.

10   Daniel Kahneman, *Thinking, Fast and Slow*. New York: Farrar, Straus, and Giroux, 2011.

11   An annotated English-language translation of the transcript of the cockpit voice data recording is available at Cockpit Voice Recorder Database, "01 June 2009–Air France 447," http://www.tailstrike.com/010609.html.

12 Ibid. This can be seen in the exchange between the pilot and copilot at the
    controls four seconds before the crash:
    02:13:40 (Robert) Climb ... climb ... climb ... climb ...
    02:13:40 (Bonin) But I've had the stick back the whole time!
    02:13:42 (Captain) No, no, no... Don't climb... no, no.

13 See, e.g., Flight Safety Foundation ALAR Tool Kit, "FSF ALAR Briefing Note 6.3:
    Terrain Avoidance (Pull-up) Maneuver," *Flight Safety Digest* (August–November
    2000), http://flightsafety.org/files/alar_bn6-3-pullup.pdf.

14 Top Koaysomboon, "Tsunami Warner Smith Dharmasaroja on a Scary Future,"
    BK: The Insider's Guide to Bangkok, December 23, 2010, http://bk.asia-city.com/
    events/article/tsunami-warner-smith-dharmasaroja-scary-future; Patrick Barta,
    "His Warning Ignored, Thai Meteorologist Now Plays Key Role," *Wall Street
    Journal*, January 10, 2005, http://www.wsj.com/articles/SB110530853574920997.

15 "Tsunami 2004 Facts and Figures," May 21, 2013, http://www.tsunami2004.net/
    tsunami-2004-facts/.

16 Anu Mittal and US Army Corps of Engineers, "Lake Pontchartrain and Vicinity
    Hurricane Protection Project," Testimony Before the Subcommittee on Energy and
    Water Development, Committee on Appropriations, House of Representatives,
    Washington, DC: US Government Accountability Office, September 28, 2005,
    http://www.gao.gov/new.items/d051050t.pdf.

17 "Complaint and Summary Judgment: Deepwater Horizon—BP Gulf of Mexico
    Oil Spill," https://www.epa.gov/enforcement/complaint-and-summary-judgment-
    deepwater-horizon-bp-gulf-mexico-oil-spill.

18 See, e.g., J. Peters and C. Büchel, "The Neural Mechanisms of Inter-temporal
    Decision-making: Understanding Variability," *Trends in Cognitive Sciences* 15, no.
    5 (2011): 227–35.

19 For a review of the historical treatment of time preferences in economics, see
    Shane Frederick, George Loewenstein, and Ted O'Donohue, "Time Discounting
    and Time Preference: A Critical Review," *Journal of Economic Literature* 40 (June
    2002): 351–401.

20 David Laibson, "Golden Eggs and Hyperbolic Discounting," *Quarterly Journal of
    Economics* 112 (2015): 443–77.

21 Grace Jean, "Indian Ocean Tsunami Warning System to Become Operational in
    2006," *National Defense*, November 2005, http://www.nationaldefensemagazine.
    org/archive/2005/November/Pages/Indian_Ocean5526.aspx.

22 See, e.g., C. Fischer, "Read This Paper Later: Procrastination with Time-Consistent
    Preferences," *Journal of Economic Behavior and Organization* 46, no. 3 (2001):
    249–69.

23 To illustrate, if instead of buying the flood proofing she invests the $10,000 in a bank at a 5% annual interest rate, after 20 years this investment will be worth $26,532. But if she pays for the improvement and after four years begins investing the $2,500 annual premium savings at the same interest rate, after 20 years this investment will be worth $59,143.

24 Yaacov Trope and Nira Liberman, "Temporal Construal," *Psychological Review* 110, no. 3 (2003): 403–21.

25 Robert J. Meyer, Earl J. Baker, Kenneth Broad, Ben Orlove, and Jeff Czykowski, "The Dynamics of Hurricane Risk Perception: Real-Time Evidence from the 2012 Atlantic Hurricane Season," *Bulletin of the American Meteorological Association* 95 (September 2014): 1389–1402.

26 Becky Oskin, "Japan Earthquake and Tsunami of 2011: Facts and Information," LiveScience, May 7, 2015, http://www.livescience.com/39110-japan-2011-earthquake-tsunami-facts.html.

27 Wikipedia, "Mikyako, Iwate," https://en.wikipedia.org/wiki/Miyako,_Iwate.

28 Edan Corkill, "Heights of Survival," *Japan Times*, June 12, 2011, 9–10.

29 Danny Lewis, "These Century-Old Stone 'Tsunami Stones' Dot Japan's Coastline," *Smithsonian Magazine*, August 31, 2015, http://www.smithsonianmag.com/smart-news/century-old-warnings-against-tsunamis-dot-japans-coastline-180956448/?no-ist.

30 A. Austin, "Galveston, The City Reclaimed: Marvelous Recuperation of a Town Wiped out Four Years Ago," *Pearson's Magazine* 13, 3 (1905): 211–19.

31 Harvey Rice, "Ike Changed Bolivar Peninsula Forever," *Houston Chronicle*, February 16, 2013.

32 E. Michel-Kerjan, S. Lemoyne de Forges, and H. Kunreuther, "Policy Tenure under the US National Flood Insurance Program (NFIP)," *Risk Analysis* 32, no. 4 (2012): 644–58.

33 Prior to 2010, the Outer Banks had encounters with storms in 2003, 2004, 2005, and 2008.

34 Ian MacKinnon, "Aceh Residents Disable Tsunami Warning System after False Alarm," *Guardian*, June 7, 2007, http://www.theguardian.com/world/2007/jun/07/indonesia.ianmackinnon.

35 K. Dow and S. L. Cutter, "Crying Wolf: Repeat Responses to Hurricane Evacuation Orders," *Coastal Management* 26 (1998): 237–52.

36 Daniel Yutzy, "ASOP 1964: Contingencies Affecting the Issuing of Public Disaster Warnings at Crescent City, California," *Research Note #4*, Disaster Research Center, Ohio State University, Columbus, OH, May 21, 1964.

37 Alison Frankel, "Double Indemnity: Was the WTC Disaster One Incident or Two?" *The American Lawyer*, September 3, 2002.

38 National Institute of Standards and Technology (NIST), "May 2003 Progress Report on the Federal Building and Fire Safety Investigation of the World Trade Center Disaster," NIST Special Publication 1000-3, 16, http://ws680.nist.gov/publication/get_pdf.cfm?pub_id=860495.

39 "History of the Twin Towers," World Trade Center (website), http://www.panynj.gov/wtcprogress/history-twin-towers.html.

40 Dan Ackman, "Larry Silverstein's $3.5B Definition," Forbes, July 23, 2003, http://www.forbes.com/2003/07/23/cx_da_0723topnews.html.

41 Chris Francescani and Scott Michels, "Who Should Pay for 9/11?" ABC News, September 10, 2007, http://abcnews.go.com/TheLaw/story?id=3579255&page=1.

42 Harry Markopolos, *No One Would Listen: A True Financial Thriller* (Hoboken: John Wiley, 2010).

43 Jennifer Fermino, "List Shock for Madoff Investors," *New York Post*, February 6, 2009, http://nypost.com/2009/02/06/list-shock-for-madoff-investors/.

44 US Securities and Exchange Commission Office of Investigations, "Investigation of the Failure of the SEC to Uncover the Bernard Madoff Ponzi Scheme," Report Number OIG-509, August 31, 2009, https://www.sec.gov/news/studies/2009/oig-509.pdf.

45 National Commission on Terrorist Attacks upon the United States, *The 9-11 Commission Report*, 2004, http://govinfo.library.unt.edu/911/report/911Report.pdf.

46 A simple approximate solution is that the probability of at least one pair is 1 minus the probability of no pairs, or 1 - (364/365) (363/365) ... (266/365) = .999.

47 The probability that we would find at least one person with our birth date from an audience of 70 is 1 minus the probability that we would find none, or 1- (364/365) ^ 70 or 17.5%.

48 An interesting footnote to the Johnny Carson story is that when he tried the problem on the audience, he misunderstood it and asked one audience member her birthday and then asked if anyone else had the same one. No one did, as this probability, of course, is small, as we've indicated.

49 See, e.g., Amos Tversky and Daniel Kahneman, "Availability: A Heuristic for Judging Frequency and Probability," *Cognitive Psychology* 5 (1973): 207–32.

50 James Ball, "How Safe Is Air Travel Really?" *Guardian*, July 24, 2014, https://www.theguardian.com/commentisfree/2014/jul/24/avoid-air-travel-mh17-math-risk-guide.

51 Garrick Blalock, Vrinda Kadiyali, and Daniel Simon, "Driving Fatalities after 9/11: A Hidden Cost of Terrorism," *Applied Economics* 41, no. 4 (2009): 1717–29.

52 Harold Maass, "The Odds Are 11 Million to 1 That You'll Die in a Plane Crash," *The Week*, July 8, 2013, http://theweek.com/articles/462449/odds-are-11-million-1-that-youll-die-plane-crash.

53 Risa Palm, Earthquake Insurance: *A Longitudinal Study of California Homeowners*, (Boulder, CO: Westview Press, 1990).

54 Risa Palm, R. and John Carroll, *Illusions of Safety: Cultural and Earthquake Hazard Response in California and Japan* (Boulder, CO: Westview Press, 1998).

55 Risk Management Solutions Inc., "When 'the Big One' Hits: 25 Years after Loma Prieta," 2014, http://rms.com/images/loma-prieta/pdf/WhenTheBigOneHits.pdf.

56 Neil Weinstein, "Unrealistic Optimism about Future Life Events," *Journal of Personality and Social Psychology* 39, no. 5 (1980): 806–20.

57 Robert J. Meyer, et al., "The Dynamics of Hurricane Risk Perception: Real-Time Evidence from the 2012 Atlantic Hurricane Season," *Bulletin of the American Meteorological Society* 95 (2014): 1389–404.

58 Ziva Kunda, "The Case for Motivated Reasoning," Psychological Bulletin, 108 (1990): 480 –98.

59 The probability that at least one attack will occur is 1 minus the probability that no attacks will occur over the course of 99 years, or $1 - .99 \wedge 99 = .63$.

60 The probability of one or more floods in 25 years is $1 - .99^{25} = .22$.

61 "Louisiana Superdome Turns Shelter," Fox News, September 16, 2004, http://www.foxnews.com/story/2004/09/16/louisiana-superdome-turns-shelter/.

62 Chris Kromm, "2010 Census reveals lingering scars of Katrina," Facing South, 2011, https://www.facingsouth.org/2011/02/2010-census-reveals-lingering-scars-of-katrina.html.

63 Eric J. Johnson, Jack C. Hershey, Jacqueline Meszaros, and Howard Kunreuther, "Framing, Probability Distortions, and Insurance Decisions," *Journal of Risk and Uncertainty* 7 (1993): 35.

64 Eric J. Johnson and Daniel Goldstein, "Do Defaults Save Lives?" *Science* 302 (2003): 1338–39.

65 Daniel Kahneman and Amos Tversky, "Prospect Theory: An Analysis of Decision under Risk" *Econometrica* 47, no. 2 (1979): 263–91.

66 Cass Sunstein, "Deciding by Default," *University of Pennsylvania Law Review* 162, no. 1 (2013).

67 William Samuelson and Richard J. Zeckhauser, "Status Quo Bias in Decision Making," *Journal of Risk and Uncertainty* 1, no. 1 (1988): 7–59.

68   National Highway Traffic Safety Administration, Quick Facts 2014, 2016. This percentage is calculated by using the 1,669 motorcyclists saved that year by wearing a helmet divided by the total number of motorcyclists killed (4,586 + 1,669).

69   Martin A Croce, Ben L. Zarzaur, Louis J. Magnotti, and Timothy C. Fabian, "Impact of Motorcycle Helmets and State Laws on Society's Burden: A National Study," *Annals of Surgery* 250, no. 3 (2009): 390–94.

70   A. J. Chapman, R. Titus, H. Ferenchick, A. Davis, and C. Rodriguez, "Repeal of the Michigan Helmet Law: Early Clinical Impacts," *American Journal of Surgery* 207, no. 3 (2014): 352–56.

71   Insurance Institute for Highway Safety Highway Loss Data, "Motorcycle Helmet Use," December 2016, http://www.iihs.org/iihs/topics/laws/helmetuse/mapmotorcyclehelmets.

72   O. Huber, R. Wider, O. W. and Huber, "Active Information Search And Complete Information Presentation In Naturalistic Risky Decision Tasks," *Acta Psychologica* 95 (1997): 15–29.

73   Robin Hogarth and Howard Kunreuther, "Decision Making Under Ignorance: Arguing with Yourself," *Journal of Risk and Uncertainty* 10 (1995): 15–38.

74   Daniel Kahneman and Amos Tversky, "Prospect Theory: An Analysis of Decision under Risk," *Econometrica* 47, no. 2 (1979): 263–91.

75   See, e.g., E. U. Weber, "Perception and Expectation Of Climate Change: Precondition For Economic And Technological Adaptation," in *Psychological Perspectives to Environmental and Ethical Issues in Management*, eds. Max Bazerman, David Messick, Ann. Tenbrunsel, and Kimberley Wade-Benzoni (San Francisco: Jossey-Bass, 1997), 314–41.

76   For an example of what is required for windstorm mitigation, see "Hurricane Mitigation Retrofits for Existing Site-Built Single-Family Residential Structures," http://consensus.fsu.edu/FBC/WMW/Reference_Document_v2rev0807.pdf.

77   See, e.g., National Hurricane Center, "Hurricane Preparedness—Be Ready," http://www.nhc.noaa.gov/prepare/ready.php.

78   Robert J. Meyer, Earl J. Baker, Kenneth Broad, Ben Orlove, and Jeff Czykowski, "The Dynamics of Hurricane Risk Perception: Real-Time Evidence from the 2012 Atlantic Hurricane Season," *Bulletin of the American Meteorological Association* 95 (September 2014): 1389–402.

79   See, e.g., Paul Fine, Ken Eames, and David L. Heymann, "Herd Immunity: A Rough Guide," *Clinical Infectious Diseases* 52, no. 7 (2001): 911–16.

80 See, e.g., David M. Burns, Lora Lee, Larry Z. Shen, Elizabeth Gilpin, H. Dennis Tollery, Jerry Vaughn, and Thomas G. Shanks, "Cigarette Smoking Behavior in the United States," in National Cancer Institute, *Smoking and Tobacco Control Monograph* No. 8 (1996), 13–42, https://cancercontrol.cancer.gov/brp/tcrb/monographs/8/index.html.

81 Alex Lo, "The Role of Social Norms in Climate Adaptation: Mediating Risk Perception and Flood Insurance Purchase," *Global Environmental Change* 23, no. 5 (2013): 1249–57.

82 Karlijin Morsink and Peter Guertz, "The Trusted Neighbor Effect: Local Experience and Demand for Microinsurance," (working paper, School of Economics, University of Oxford, 2012).

83 Howard Kunreuther et al., *Disaster Insurance Protection: Public Policy Lessons* (New York: Wiley InterScience, 1978).

84 De la Herrán-Arita, Alberto K., et al., "CD4+ T cell autoimmunity to hypocretin/orexin and cross-reactivity to a 2009 H1N1 influenza A epitope in narcolepsy," *Science Translational Medicine*, 5 (2013): 216.

85 Heidi Ledford, "Journal retracts paper linking vaccine and narcolepsy," newsblog, July 31, 2014, http://blogs.nature.com/news/2014/07/journal-retracts-paper-linking-vaccine-and-narcolepsy.html.

86 Jeffrey Baker, "The Pertussis Vaccine Controversy in Great Britain, 1974–1986," *Vaccine* 21 (2003): 4003–10.

87 E. J. Gangarosa, A. M. Galazka, C. R. Wolfe, L. M. Phillips, R. E. Gangarosa, E. Miller, et al. "Impact of Anti-vaccine Movements on Pertussis Control: The Untold Story," *Lancet* 351 (1998): 356–61.

88 H. Coulter and B. L. Fisher, *A Shot in the Dark* (San Diego: Harcourt Brace Jovanovich, 1985).

89 Jeffrey Baker, "The Pertussis Vaccine Controversy in Great Britain, 1974–1986," *Vaccine* 21 (2003): 4003–10.

90 Matthieu Domenech de Cellès, Felicia M. G. Magpantay, Aaron A. King, Pejman Rohani, "The Pertussis Enigma: Reconciling Epidemiology, Immunology and Evolution," *Proceedings of the Royal Society of London: Biological Sciences*, January 13, 2016.

91 D. J. Isenberg, "Group Polarization: A Critical Review and Meta-Analysis," *Journal of Personality and Social Psychology* 50, no. 6 (1986): 1141–51.

92 H. Kunreuther, R. J. Meyer, and Erwann Michel-Kejan, "Strategies for Better Protection Against Catastrophic Risks" in *Behavioral Perspectives on Public Policy*, ed. E. Shafir (Princeton, NJ: Princeton University Press, 2012), 398–416.

93 R. Thaler and C. Sunstein, *Nudge: The Gentle Power of Choice Architecture* (New Haven, CT: Yale University Press, 2008).

94   P. Slovic, B. Fischhoff, and S. Lichtenstein, "Accident Probabilities and Seat Belt Usage: A Psychological Perspective," *Accident Analysis and Prevention* 10 (1978): 281–85.

95   N. D. Weinstein, K. Kolb, and B. D. Goldstein, "Using Time Intervals Between Expected Events to Communicate Risk Magnitudes," *Risk Analysis* 16, no. 3 (1996): 305–8.

96   H. Kunreuther, N. Novemsky, and D. Kahneman, "Making Low Probabilities Useful," *Journal of Risk and Uncertainty* 23 (2001): 103–20.

97   B. C. Madrian and D. F. Shea, "The Power of Suggestion: Inertia in 401(k) Participation and Savings Behavior," *Quarterly Journal of Economics* 16 (2001): 1149–87; R. H. Thaler and S. Benartzi, "Save More Tomorrow™: Using Behavioral Economics to Increase Employee Saving," Journal of Political Economy 112, no. S1 (2004): S164-87.

98   As an illustration in the case of Florida, see "Flood Resistant Construction and the 2010 Florida Building Code," January 2012, https://www.charlottecountyfl.gov/services/buildingconstruction/Documents/BASF-FloodProvisions.pdf.

99   H. Kunreuther and E. Michel-Kerjan, "Demand for Fixed-Price Multi-Year Contracts: Experimental Evidence from Insurance Decisions," *Journal of Risk and Uncertainty* 51 (2015): 171–94.

100   Insurance Institute for Property Loss Reduction (IIPLR), *Homes and Hurricanes: Public Opinion Concerning Various Issues Relating to Home Builders, Building Codes and Damage Mitigation* (Boston, MA: IIPLR, 1995).

101   Nathanial Gronewold, "Risk: Hurricane-Smashed Texas Barrier Island is a Magnet for New Development; Defenses Remain Pending," *ClimateWire*, March 11, 2015, http://www.eenews.net/stories/1060014803.

102   Jonathan Gregory, "Projections of Sea Level Rise," in *Climate Change* 2013: The Physical Science Basis, chapter 13 of the 2013 IPCC Fifth Assessment Report, https://www.ipcc.ch/pdf/unfccc/cop19/3_gregory13sbsta.pdf.

103   Joey Flechas and Jenny Staletovich, "Miami Beach's Battle to Stem Rising Tides," *Miami Herald*, October 23, 2015, http://www.miamiherald.com/news/local/community/miami-dade/miami-beach/article41141856.html.

104   Andrew Rice, "When Will New York City Sink?" *New York Magazine*, September 5, 2016.

105   H. Kunreuther and E. Michel-Kerjan, *At War with the Weather: Managing Large-Scale Risks in a New Era of Catastrophes* (Cambridge, MA: MIT Press, 2011).

106   Jacob Vigdor, "The Economic Aftermath of Hurricane Katrina," *Journal of Economic Perspectives* 22, no. 4 (2008): 135–54.

107 H. Kunreuther, R. J. Meyer, and E. Michel-Kerjan, "Overcoming Decision Biases to Reduce Losses from Natural Catastrophes," in *Behavioral Foundations of Policy*, ed. E. Shafir (Princeton, NJ: Princeton University Press, 2013).

108 Harvey Rice, "Ike Changed Bolivar Peninsula Forever," *Houston Chronicle*, February 16, 2013, http://www.houstonchronicle.com/news/houston-texas/houston/article/Ike-changed-Bolivar-Peninsula-forever-4285143.php.

109 Associated Press–NORC Center for Public Affairs Research, "After a Disaster Strikes: Public Opinion on Rebuilding and Relocation Policies," July 2013, http://www.apnorc.org/PDFs/Resilience%20in%20Superstorm%20Sandy/AP-NORC%20Sandy%20Issue%20Brief.pdf.

110 For more details on this managed retreat in Staten Island, see Elizabeth Rush, "As the Seas Rise" *New Republic*, October 25, 2015, http://newrepublic.com/article/123182/managing-retreat-along-new-york-citys-coasts.

111 New Jersey Dept. of Environmental Protection, "Frequently Asked Questions: Superstorm Sandy Blue Acres Buyout Program," http://www.nj.gov/dep/greenacres/pdf/faqs-blueacres.pdf.

112 The H. John Heinz III Center for Science, Economics, and the Environment, *The Hidden Costs of Coastal Hazards* (Washington, DC: Island Press, 1999).

113 PlaNYC, *A Stronger, More Resilient New York* (New York: City of New York, 2013).

114 Carolyn Kousky and H. Kunreuther, "Addressing Affordability in the National Flood Insurance Program," *Journal of Extreme Events* 1, no. 1 (2014): 11–28.

115 National Research Council, *Affordability of National Flood Insurance Program Premiums—Report 1*, (Washington, DC: National Academies Press, 2015).

Index

About the Authors

Robert Meyer is the Frederick H. Ecker/MetLife Insurance Professor of Marketing and codirector, Wharton Risk Management and Decision Processes Center. His work has appeared in a wide variety of professional journals and books, including the *Journal of Consumer Research*; *Journal of Marketing Research*; *Journal of Risk and Uncertainty*; *Marketing Science*; *Management Science*; and *Risk Analysis*.

Howard Kunreuther is the James G. Dinan Professor of Decision Sciences and Public Policy and codirector, Wharton Risk Management and Decision Processes Center. His recent books include *At War with the Weather* (with Erwann Michel-Kerjan), winner of the Kulp-Wright Book Award from the American Risk and Insurance Association in 2011; *Insurance and Behavioral Economics: Improving Decisions in the Most Misunderstood Industry* (with Mark Pauly and Stacey McMorrow); and *Leadership Dispatches: Chile's Extraordinary Comeback from Disaster* (with Michael Useem and Erwann Michel-Kerjan).

About Wharton Digital Press

Wharton Digital Press was established to inspire bold, insightful thinking within the global business community. In the tradition of The Wharton School of the University of Pennsylvania and its online business journal, Knowledge@Wharton, Wharton Digital Press uses innovative digital technologies to help managers meet the challenges of today and tomorrow.

As an entrepreneurial publisher, Wharton Digital Press delivers relevant, accessible, conceptually sound, and empirically based business knowledge to readers wherever and whenever they need it. Its format ranges from ebooks to print books available through print-on-demand technology. Directed to a general business audience, the Press's areas of interest include management and strategy, innovation and entrepreneurship, finance and investment, leadership, marketing, operations, human resources, social responsibility, business–government relations, and more.

wdp.wharton.upenn.edu

About The Wharton School

The Wharton School of the University of Pennsylvania—founded in 1881 as the first collegiate business school—is recognized globally for intellectual leadership and ongoing innovation across every major discipline of business education. The most comprehensive source of business knowledge in the world, Wharton bridges research and practice through its broad engagement with the global business community. The School has 5,000 undergraduate, MBA, executive MBA, and doctoral students; nearly 9,200 annual participants in executive education programs; and an alumni network of 94,000 graduates.

wdp.wharton.upenn.edu

CPSIA information can be obtained
at www.ICGtesting.com
Printed in the USA
FSHW02n1944140918
52313FS

9 781613 630808